Homespun Christmas

Treasured family recipes, memories,
homemade decorations, heart-felt gifts
and holiday traditions

To:

From:

"A Country Store In Your Mailbox" ℠

Gooseberry Patch
149 Johnson Drive
Department BOOK
Delaware, OH 43015

★

1·800·85·GOOSE
1-800·854·6673

Copyright 1996, Gooseberry Patch 1-888052-00-7
First Printing 40,000 copies, June 1996
Second Printing 30,000 copies, June 1997

How to Subscribe

Would you like to receive
"A Country Store In Your Mailbox" ℠?
For a 2-year subscription to our
Gooseberry Patch catalog,
simply send $3.00 to:

Gooseberry Patch
P.O. Box 190 Dept. BOOK
Delaware, OH 43015

♲ This book is printed on recycled paper.

Printed in the United States of America

Contents

DEDICATION

To each and every one of our Gooseberry Friends
who have generously shared treasured family recipes
and heart-felt memories.

IN APPRECIATION

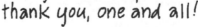

To all of our Contributing Editors who took
time in their busy lives to share their gifts
of creativity for this special edition...
thank you, one and all!

Memories

Grandmother's Pin

This is for anyone who misses a loved one around the holidays...
I like to wear my grandmother's Christmas pin. It's a nice way
to remember her and to feel like she's still a part of our holidays.

Glenda Hill

Bird Messengers

Have your kids ever asked you how Santa knows if they're naughty
or nice? In our house, the answer was easy. The birds knew.
All year long the birds keep a watch over all the children of the world.
We all know that the animals can talk to Santa, so the birds can fly to
the North Pole and report their findings. Birds can be sitting high in a
tree and watching you play in the yard, or they can peek in your window
to see if you went to bed on time or did the chores you were told. In
our home we always had a bird feeder out the moment the weather
turned cold. Remember, the birds are messengers for Santa Claus!

Wendy Lee Paffenroth

The Real Santa Claus

Santa Claus was as real to me back when I was a child as he is today. He was a kind and caring person who always knew the best present to give. It wasn't always what we would ask for, but always a gift given with love. I have special memories of my dad having a talk with me when I began to doubt that Santa really existed. My dad confirmed that Santa was and always would exist as long as there is love to share, a child somewhere to share it with, and the willingness to give of yourself an unexpected gift from your heart to someone each holiday season.

Juanita Williams

Midnight Mass

For us, there is nothing more special than going to Midnight Mass as a family and hearing the music and choir at their Christmas best. The trumpets and singing make it a magical moment. Music is good throughout the year, but it's never as magical and wonderful as on Christmas Eve.

Barb McFaden

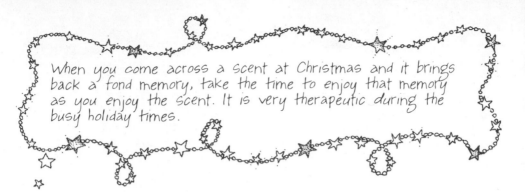

When you come across a scent at Christmas and it brings back a fond memory, take the time to enjoy that memory as you enjoy the scent. It is very therapeutic during the busy holiday times.

The Gingerbread House

My three grandchildren were coming to Texas from Georgia for the Christmas holidays. I was cooking and baking and wrapping gifts, scheming to give them a wonderful Christmas memory to take home with them. I decided this year it would be a gingerbread house. I shaped and cut and baked the house "pieces" ahead of time. I bought an assortment of candies and prepared meringue powder to use as glue for building the houses. My three grandsons arrived, and with their mother's help and mine, they began to assemble the houses and decorate them. We all had a wonderful time, but as we cleaned up the mess, I wondered if the day would really qualify as a Christmas memory. That evening, as we watched a new children's video, I missed young Frank and went to look for him. There in the kitchen, walking around and around the table that held the finished gingerbread houses, was my middle grandson. His eyes were shining and filled with wonder as he looked at the beautiful gingerbread house he had built. He looked at me and said, "Oh, can I please take it home with me?" That's when I knew the day really qualified as a Christmas memory.

Tamara Gruber

Bird Feeder Pine Cones

Have you and your children ever gathered pine cones and then not known what to do with them? In our house, we make bird feeders. Grandma buys some peanut butter & some sunflower seeds. We lay out newspaper on the table and then tie a string about 2 feet long to the top of the pine cone. Sometimes we have to wrap it around the cone a bit to hold. Then we put on rubber gloves and take a butter knife and push the peanut butter all over the cone. Next we fill up an old coffee can about half full of sunflower seeds, put in the peanut butter-covered cone, snap on the lid of the can, and shake it. Then when we take the pine cone out, we press the sunflower seeds into the peanut butter until it's all covered. Wrap in wax paper and tie with a ribbon. You can give them to the neighbors to hang in their trees. Make sure you do this when the weather is cold. If you hang these above 45 degrees, the peanut butter might run off. This can be done with wild bird seed too, but we have found the sunflower seeds attract more cardinals and songbirds. Kids, make sure you help clean up the mess!

Wendy Lee Paffenroth

Snapshot Saver

If you know older people in a nursing home or in a small apartment, have someone cut a piece of plexiglass to fit the top of a dresser. Take all the family photos, Christmas snapshots, even Christmas cards or birthday cards and place them under the plexiglass face up. It's a nice collage of photos that means a lot. Every time that person goes to her dresser, she will see happy memories of loved ones. My mom has always had this on her dresser.

Wendy Lee Paffenroth

Long Ago Christmas

by Doris Connell

Long ago, at Christmas time, how thrilled we all would be
When our dad would say to us, "Let's go and find our tree."
What fun we'd have looking for a very special kind;
It must be the finest tree that we could possibly find.

They were all so lovely, throughout the woodland scene,
But at last we'd come upon a beautiful evergreen.
We'd start for home, so gaily, carrying our chosen tree.
We could hardly wait until our mom, back home, could see.

The lovely tree went on a stand after we were tucked in bed,
And all the dreams of Christmas would fill each sleepy head.
Ah, then, on Christmas morning, what a glorious, lovely sight!
It seemed a group of fairies had worked there through the night.

For all the lovely branches were full of so many things:
Glowing candles and tinsel, popcorn and peppermint canes.
We still have a Christmas that is beautiful in every way,
But memories of those long ago, are in our hearts to stay.

Submitted by Juanita Williams

A Special Ornament

Our big family has always been very close. Christmas was the day we all gathered together at my grandparents' house. After I married, we moved 1,500 miles away. I missed my family terribly. One year my husband had a business trip near my grandparents' city. He went to their house for the annual holiday get-together. When he got ready to leave, Grandma reached up high on their Christmas tree and took off an old glass bird ornament with a feathered brush tail. It had hung on their tree for as long as I could remember. She sent it home with him for me. Many years have since passed, but each year I take the lovely old bird from its box and reverently place it on our Christmas tree. Someday it will be passed on to one of my daughters, who will love it and cherish it as much as I have.

Nancy Campbell

Blessed are the children

who have parents and grandparents who can relate the stories of their own pasts, connecting the younger with the older memories, lighting a taper in the imagination that never goes out.

Juanita Williams

Christmas Tree Outing

Instead of buying your tree already cut, get a forest permit and take time to go to the woods and pick one out. We have done this for the past ten years; we go the weekend after Thanksgiving. We used to go only as a family, but through the years we have gotten other families interested and it has become a major event. We pack the kids up along with treats and hot cocoa, and off we go! By cutting our own tree in the woods, we end up with a fresher tree that lasts longer. It takes hours finding that perfect tree, and we usually pick out 15 to 30 before we find that special tree. Each year we find one that is better than last year's.

Barb McFaden

Tradition of Joy

A Christmas tradition in our house that we have held faithfully since I was a child goes like this: Every Christmas morning when I was young, my brothers and sisters and I were not allowed to come down and see what was under the tree until Dad and Mom were ready...we waited on the top stair until we heard our cue: *Joy to the World* blasting from the stereo at top volume. Then we knew Christmas could begin. We went careening down the stairs to behold a wonderland of toys and magic. To this day, although the kids are in their teens... and they say, "Oh Mom, *do* we have to wait for *Joy to the World*?"...they still know that they can't come downstairs until it is blasting on our stereo. As silly as it sounds, it never fails to bring a tear to my eye to this day.

Barb McFaden

Little Girls' Songs

Picture two little girls in the year 1905, skipping along on their way to school and singing to the first snowflakes of the winter:

*Old woman, old woman, old woman up high
She's plucking her geese, see the white feathers fly!*

These little girls were my mother and my aunt.

Pat Akers

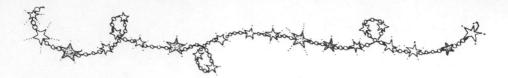

Happiness sneaks in through a door you didn't know you left open.

John Barrymore

Family Memories Journal

When someone you love becomes a new mother, buy her a large, bound blank journal and write several family recipes in it. Instruct her to keep adding her child's favorite recipes to the book... favorite cookies, meals, and so forth. Then, the first year that the child has left home, gotten married or moved away, wrap this book up and give it to them. Be sure to add the family holiday traditions, and you will give a gift of love that has no price tag. You can also have other close relatives write in a favorite recipe that maybe your child loved when they visited there. Not only will they have the recipe, but a wonderful sample of "Aunt Linda's" handwriting to remember her by. This is a Christmas present that you cannot buy, because it takes years to gather. It's a way of showing how much your child is loved. I have books for both of my children.

Wendy Lee Paffenroth

Try keeping a "next year" journal. Tell yourself what to do differently next year, or make lists of places to go, people to see and things to do that you never got to do this year. Review your notes once in a while during the year so you don't forget again next year. You can plan to do a lot more when you know what it is you want to accomplish!

Christmas Book Collection

Parents with small children, this is for you. When we were growing up my parents bought a new Christmas book for each of us around the middle of November. After the holidays, the books went into a box in the attic. Each year we added to the collection, and I can remember as a child asking my mom to bring down the Christmas box of books as soon as Thanksgiving was over. I kept the collection and added to it when my children were small. Many are tales not found any longer. Our favorite story was "Granny Glittens and Her Amazing Mittens." Each night we would have a story read to us up until Christmas Eve.

Wendy Lee Paffenroth

Start a collection of Christmas books to hand down over the years. Books with Christmas themes, illustrations, stories, poems, recipes...old and new...will be treasured over the years. You can search new and used bookstores, garage sales and tag sales. The older books are becoming scarce, but occasionally you can find delightful old treasuries of Christmas stories. Bring the books out every December to enjoy and share with family.

Nancie Gensler

Christmas Lights Outing

On Christmas Eve, we always pack the kids in our van and go look at Christmas light displays in our city and the suburbs. We have hot cocoa and a special spicy popcorn snack in the car with Christmas carols in the tape deck. Something so simple can be an event if you make it that way.

Yvonne Van Brimmer

Heather's Long Ago "Christmas Coffee"

Heather's house was a large and wonderful 100-year-old farm home filled with family heirlooms and antiques. I was Heather's childhood friend and had spent many after-school hours, preteen sleepovers and birthday parties in that house. However, there was never an event like the traditional family "Christmas Coffee." Those lucky enough to be invited never declined their invitations. Since I was Heather's friend, and friends need moral support at such "grown-up" functions, I was invited. The house was truly the stuff dreams are made of that day. It was absolute grandeur and magic. The large dining room had many lovely antique cupboards filled with beautiful patterned china, gleaming crystal, wonderful coffee pots, teapots, pitchers, and sugar bowls. The large table was laden with treats. Some of the most delectable ones were the fresh, homemade doughnuts. The doughnut recipe had been used in this county for well over 100 years, passed from generation to generation. Toppings held in china bowls and pitchers were powdered sugar, grated coconut, cinnamon sugar, chocolate sauce, and even maple syrup. Coffee was accompanied by whipped cream, brandy, shaved bittersweet chocolate, and even Irish whiskey. (Of course, at my age I stuck to the whipped cream!) So here I was, with all the "Big Ladies" in town dressed in their finery, drinking and eating from all these heavenly china pieces. It was, at least through a child's eyes, just like a dream. I felt special that day, and I believe every other guest felt that way. I know that the Christmas spirit enveloped the entire house. That "Christmas Coffee" is a wonderful memory (even though almost 35 years have passed) and a tradition which I hope still lives on at Heather's family home.

Judy Hand

Memory Tree

We started when we were first married. Whenever my husband and I went somewhere, we either took photos or bought a memento that was small enough to turn into a tree ornament. Twenty years later, we reminisce about our great life together as we hang the ornaments we have gathered over the years.

Wendy Lee Paffenroth

Personalized Christmas Ornaments

Seems like everyone buys a baby ornament with "Baby's First Christmas" on it, but in our house the tradition goes on every year. I have purchased two golden ornaments, each engraved for my son Jim and daughter Sue, every year. I have also purchased one for my husband and myself. I have the names and dates put on them. Sometimes I try to find one that will bring back special memories, such as a train ornament for the year Jim got his train set, or a rocket for the year he went to Space Camp. Sue has a ballerina for the year she was in the "big show" and a nativity ornament for the year she was "Mary" in the church play. Some years we even put nicknames on them. These ornaments can usually be bought for a few dollars at the local department stores. My mom did this with me, and at my bridal shower I received a whole boxful of ornaments, each with a special memory attached. Don't forget to put the date on the ornament somewhere, even on the bottom. When a child moves from home, gather their personal ornaments together and present them for their very first tree. It's a gift that can't be duplicated.

Wendy Lee Paffenroth

My Best-Ever Christmas Present

I t was the Christmas of 1941, bleak even for a child because World War II was a mere eighteen days old and no one knew how it would all end. I was 8 years old that year and all I wanted for Christmas was a REAL 14-karat gold-filled wristwatch. Christmas Eve arrived; my dad came in the house with lots of packages for my mother, and one gigantic gift-wrapped box for me. I adored my father and I tried so hard to hide my massive disappointment about the size of that box. I wasn't going to get my watch after all. Christmas morning came, and I searched among the packages for a small box addressed to me. Even Santa hadn't left me a small box. My dad passed out the presents, saving the big box until last. When he placed it in front of me, I began to unwrap it, trying oh-so-hard not to show my disappointment. To my confusion, when the box was opened there was another box inside...all beautifully gift-wrapped and containing... another box. To my child's mind, it seemed those boxes went on forever. With each smaller box hope grew within me, until finally I opened a package with a jewelry box inside. There, on the velvet lining, ✰✰ lay my golden wristwatch. My dad took the watch from me and showed me something very special. If you held the watch at just the right angle, you could see two tiny diamond chips; one on either side of the watch face. I have had many Christmases since then and have received many wonderful...and much more valuable...gifts than that wristwatch, but in my memory, and for all time, that watch shall remain my "best ever" gift.

Tamara Gruber

One of the lovely ways of making Christmas the glowing occasion it should be is to use it as a special time of kind deeds.

Juanita Williams

A Ring Becomes A Reminder

It was a short time before Christmas, back in the '40's, when we lived in Florida on the Bartow Air Base. My dad was stationed in the Philippines, and we hadn't seen him for a year. How happy we were to hear he was finally coming home. My mother was very excited and busy making Christmas cookies and holiday goodies, as well as cleaning everything until our little house sparkled. We helped set up a small Christmas tree on a corner table in the living room, decorating it with blue lights, angel hair and icicles. The day finally came when Dad arrived home in his starched uniform, bringing pretty Christmas packages for Mother and the three of us. Dad called each child aside, giving us a special coming-home present. He gave me a tiny gold ring with a red ruby center and told me to always take special care of the ring because he had bought in it the Philippines and it couldn't be replaced. I put the ring on and felt so special, running all around the neighborhood showing my beautiful ring to my friends.

The next thing I knew, the ring was missing from my finger...it was lost! I looked everywhere, but the ring was never to be found. How I dreaded telling my dad and the rest of the family that I had lost my red ruby ring. I remember hiding around by the fireplace and crying and crying. I could hear my mother calling me, asking if anyone knew where I was. My brother finally found me, and everyone found out what had happened. My dad tried to dry my tears and he told me that Santa Claus knows everything, and if I really tried to be a good girl from now until Christmas, maybe he would bring me a new ring. Christmas morning arrived, and we had some special gifts to open, but the tiny box under the tree marked "to Judy from Santa" was what I opened first. There, sparkling in the blue Christmas lights, was another tiny gold ring with a ruby center. I'll never forget the happiness I felt at that moment. My dad is gone now, and over the years the sparkling ruby fell out, but I still have the tiny gold ring to remind me of that happy Christmas morning years ago.

Judy Borecky

Christmas is for Pets, Too!

Every holiday season we include our pets. The hamster gets a nibble treat and pretty bows on her cage (out of reach of her chewing mouth). Our dog and friends' dogs get our homemade doggie biscuits and a red ribbon for their collars. The cat gets a calico catnip-stuffed heart or a mouse-shaped toy and a bow briefly on her collar as she pulls it off and plays with it within minutes. (Makes for great pictures!) It's very difficult to get a bow on a fish, but we decorate the tank with tinsel and ribbon...even those plastic removable decals look cute. Our two youngest boys have tree frogs in an aquarium (we call it "the swamp"...) and it, too, can be festooned with ribbon and an extra helping of crickets from the pet store. Don't forget to adorn "Tweetie's" cage, either!

Yvonne Van Brimmer

Family Christmas Puzzle

When the Christmas things start appearing in the stores, pick up a 500-piece puzzle with a pretty Christmas or holiday picture. Set up a card table in the corner of a room and put it out over the Thanksgiving holiday. Younger kids can find the smooth-edged pieces, or just turn them all right side up. The idea is to do the puzzle by Christmas Eve. When you feel stressed with the holidays, go put a few pieces in place. Whenever you walk by or the kids have "nothing to do," add a few pieces. You will be surprised that even the dads get involved, and before long the puzzle is taking shape. I bought one showing a village all decked out for the holidays. Each shop is decorated differently, and it's such fun to complete it shop by shop. This is a great stress-reliever, even if you only take 5 or 10 minutes a day to work on it.

Wendy Lee Paffenroth

A New Christmas Tradition

Start a new Christmas tradition for your family. There are many books in the library that describe holiday traditions from around the world. It's a wonderful learning tool to teach children about their own ethnic traditions, as well as those traditions from other cultures. It will teach them to appreciate those whose backgrounds are different from their own. My husband's family came here from Germany long ago. After a little research, I now prepare Christ Stollen for Christmas morning breakfast. It's a delicious sweet bread that depicts the Baby Jesus wrapped in swaddling clothes. I have a friend named Lucia who loves to celebrate St. Lucia's Day on December 13th. I love to bake and sometimes give her Lussekatter Buns as a gift (a Swedish tradition). Many of our December celebrations from around the world are concerned with bringing light into a darkened world. Have fun and share your knowledge with a child.

Tamara Gruber

Memory Book

When older family members, such as grandparents or great aunts and uncles, are visiting for the holidays, keep a guest book handy and ask them to write a page or two of their favorite memories as a child. What was Christmas like at their home? Can they recall their favorite Christmas? Perhaps they could write their favorite recipe in the book for a holiday treat. Your memory book can be packed away each year with the Christmas ornaments, and placed out on the coffee table the next year. It's fun to read and recall best memories of those loved ones and their good old days.

Juanita Williams

Alta Miller's Popcorn Balls

Christmas memories are ever so sweet at our house. For as long as I can remember, we never had a Christmas Eve without Mom making up a batch of her special recipe popcorn balls. With four children in the family and cousins galore, we would gather 'round to wait for Mom to cook up the syrup as we enjoyed making batches of her favorite treat! Her basic recipe follows, but she made each batch special, sometimes red; sometimes green. We tried blue ones and yellow ones; even added walnuts and bits of candied fruit.

As a young child it was such great fun to wait around a huge batch of popcorn, buttering up our little hands to help make these special treats. Each year we joined in the fun. We'd wrap them in clear wrap, tie them with Christmas ribbon, and put them in a big basket near the tree. Most often, as in years past, this is our gift to family and friends. I have to admit, even though I am grown with four children of own, I still depend on Mom to ready the syrup, and I enjoy buttering hands with my children and molding the popcorn balls. I have been blessed with a special mom, and I know that when the popcorn balls are ready, it's time for Christmas!

1 c. sugar
1/3 c. corn syrup
1/3 c. water
1/4 c. butter

1/2 t. salt
1/2 t. cream of tartar
Optional: green & red
     food coloring, walnuts,
     candied fruit

Combine all ingredients. Cook to hard crack stage. Add optional food coloring to make Christmas-colored balls. Pour over 8 cups popped corn and mix thoroughly. Grease hands with butter and mold into balls. The mixture will be hot. Little ones should be careful not to burn hands while molding. You can add candied fruit or walnuts for variety.

Juanita Williams

Caroling Parties

You're Invited

Please come

Welcome

eck The halls

Festive Foods

and Glorious Feasts

Fa la la la

A man hath no better thing under the sun than to eat and to drink and to be merry.

Ecclesiastes 8:15

R.S.V.P.

Let It Snow

Much Cheer!

Kiss the Cook

Great Beginnings

Country Cheese and Cider Spread

These cheese "apples" are fun to do and add flair to your party.

8-oz. pkg. cream cheese,
  softened
1/2 c. apple cider
1/2 lb. Swiss cheese,
  shredded

1/2 lb. Cheddar cheese,
  shredded
1 stick butter, melted
paprika and parsley for
  garnish

Soften cream cheese and beat until smooth. Add apple cider, Swiss and Cheddar cheeses, and butter. Beat until fluffy. Mound this mixture into 3 buttered cups or containers, mounding tops. Chill overnight in refrigerator. Remove chilled cheese from containers and mold each mound into the shape of an apple. Cut stems from real apples and press into each "cheese apple." Coat each cheese apple with paprika. Serve on a parsley-covered plate with crackers and fresh fruit.

Ginger Cheese Ball

A really different, sweet spread.

8 oz. dates, pitted
6 or 8 pieces candied ginger
1/2 c. pecans

2 8-oz. pkgs. cream cheese
flaked coconut

Chop dates, ginger and nuts in food processor. Add cheese and blend. Shape into a large ball and cover with flaked coconut. Surround with gingersnaps.

> Who says you have to have a sit-down dinner on Christmas Eve? You can be informal and have hors d'oeuvres and desserts...much easier to prepare and a very relaxed atmosphere.

Festive Tropical Fruit Dip

The coffee liqueur gives it the taste of the tropics.

2 eggs, beaten
1/4 c. honey
1/4 c. orange juice

1/2 c. plus 1 T. coffee liqueur
1 c. cream, whipped

Pour first four ingredients into a saucepan. Cook over low heat, stirring constantly until mixture coats spoon. Cool. Fold cooled mixture into whipped cream. Serve with sliced fresh fruit such as bananas, strawberries and pineapple.

Makes approximately 2-1/2 cups of dip.

Tangy Cheese in a Round of Rye

A great appetizer for your holiday potluck.

1-1/2 lbs. sharp Cheddar
   cheese, grated
1/4 lb. blue cheese
1 t. dry mustard
2 T. butter, softened
1 t. Worcestershire sauce
2 t. onion or chives, grated

12-oz. bottle of beer
3 to 5 lb. loaf of rye
   (round or oval shaped)
loaf of party rye
paprika
parsley

Place first 6 ingredients in a bowl to soften, at least 30 minutes or longer. Add beer slowly and beat until smooth and fluffy. Hollow out the loaf of bread (reserve to thinly slice for the dip). Sawtooth the crust as you would a watermelon. Fill bread bowl with this mix, garnish with paprika and parsley, and refrigerate. Serve on a big bread board with the reserved, sliced rye from center of loaf and extra party rye loaf.

Serves 20 to 30.

Rudolph's Nose Herbal Chili Ball

Make ahead of time to allow flavors to blend.

8-oz. pkg. cream cheese,
   softened
8 oz. sharp Cheddar cheese,
   grated
2 t. chili powder
1/2 t. thyme

1/4 t. rosemary
1 t. poppy seeds
1 t. sesame seeds
2 t. grated onion
1 garlic clove, minced
1 t. sherry

Mix cheeses together, add remaining ingredients and thoroughly beat. This can be done in a food processor until smooth. Refrigerate this mixture for 30 minutes, or until the mixture can be handled easily. Shape into a ball or a log. Roll in chili powder until coated. Wrap in wax paper, then place in a plastic bag. Refrigerate at least 24 hours before serving. Serve with crackers.

Makes a one-pound cheese ball.

Almond Punch

Just right for a big party...use as a mixer, too.

4 c. water
6 c. sugar
4 3-oz. pkgs. lemon gelatin
6-oz. can frozen orange juice
   concentrate, thawed

6-oz. can frozen lemonade
   concentrate, thawed
2 large cans pineapple juice
1-1/2 oz. almond extract
4 qts. ginger ale

Combine water and sugar and cook until syrupy. Add gelatin and dissolve. Add fruit juices, one gallon water and almond extract. Let stand until ready to use. Pour 1/8 of juice mixture over ice in punch bowl; add 1/2 quart ginger ale. Continue adding ingredients in the same proportions to punch bowl as needed.

Serves 100.

Hot Pecan Dip

Hearty flavor and texture in a nutty, toasted appetizer.

1/2 c. pecans, chopped
2 T. butter, melted
1/2 t. salt
2 T. milk
2-1/2 oz. dried beef, chopped

1/4 c. green pepper, chopped
1 small onion, grated
1/4 t. pepper
1/2 t. garlic powder
1/2 c. sour cream

Mix first three ingredients. Bake at 350 degrees for 15 minutes. Remove from oven and set aside. Mix milk, dried beef, green pepper, onion, pepper, and garlic powder. Fold sour cream into milk mixture. Pour into a 9-inch baking dish (preferably a quiche dish) and sprinkle with the pecan mixture. Bake at 350 degrees for 20 minutes. Serve this hot with party pumpernickel bread or with crackers.

Crab Quiche Appetizers

Set these out and watch them disappear!

1 pkg. pie crusts (15 oz.)
8 oz. crab flakes or chunks
4 eggs, beaten
1-1/2 c. half and half

1/4 t. dill weed
1-1/2 c. Swiss cheese, shredded
1/2 c. Parmesan cheese

Preheat oven to 450 degrees. Unfold and gently roll out both pie crusts. Arrange crusts slightly overlapping to cover bottom and sides of a greased 15"x10" jelly roll pan. Crimp edges; prick bottom and sides. Bake 10 to 12 minutes or until golden brown. Reduce oven temperature to 350 degrees. Cover bottom of crust with seafood. Mix eggs, half and half, and dill until blended. Add cheeses and pour over seafood. Bake 30 minutes. Cut into squares.

Yield: approximately 5 dozen appetizers.

Cheese Sausage Squares

Careful! You might spoil your dinner!

2 15-oz. refrigerated pie crusts
1 lb. pork sausage
2 c. green peppers, chopped
2 c. onion, chopped
2 4-1/2 oz. jars
    mushrooms, drained
1 c. Parmesan cheese

1 t. each: dried basil, garlic
    powder, dried oregano,
    crushed red pepper
16-oz. pkg. American cheese
    slices
2 c. tomatoes, chopped

Preheat oven to 450 degrees. Unfold and gently roll out both pie crusts. Arrange crusts, slightly overlapping, to cover bottom and side of greased 15"x10" jelly roll pan. Crimp edges; prick bottom and sides. Bake 10 to 12 minutes. Cook sausage in skillet, add peppers and onions and sauté until tender. Drain. Stir in mushrooms, seasonings, and 1/2 cup Parmesan cheese. Place 15 American cheese slices on top, slightly overlapping, to cover crust. Top with filling and remaining cheese slices. Sprinkle with tomato and remaining Parmesan cheese. Bake 10 minutes. Cool 15 minutes. Cut into 1-1/2 inch squares.

Approximately 5 dozen appetizers.

Fast & Fun Holiday Sausage Stars

When you need something quick and tasty!

1 lb. pkg. sausage,
    cooked, drained
    and crumbled
8 oz. Swiss cheese, grated
juice of 1 lemon

1 t. garlic, finely minced
1/2 t. dried thyme
1/2 c. mayonnaise
1 loaf white bread, thinly sliced
paprika

Combine first six ingredients and stir well. Using stars, trees, or other holiday cookie cutters, cut shapes out of bread slices. Lightly toast. Place a heaping tablespoon of mixture on each bread shape. Sprinkle with paprika. Broil 3 to 5 minutes or until cheese melts and bubbles slightly.

Mulled Cranberry Cider

Tangy cranberry, warm and inviting.

1 small orange
8 c. cranberry-raspberry drink
1/4 c. light brown sugar
orange peel cut into strips

6" cinnamon stick
1 t. whole cloves
1 star anise

Using a vegetable peeler, remove orange peel and set aside. Squeeze the juice from the orange, discard seed and pulp. In a large saucepan combine cranberry-raspberry drink and brown sugar. In an 8-inch square of cheesecloth, combine most of the orange peel strips, cinnamon, whole cloves, and star anise. Tie cheesecloth with cotton twine. Add to liquid. Bring mixture to boiling; reduce heat. Cover and simmer for 10 minutes. Remove from heat and discard spices. Serve warm, garnished with additional orange peel.

Quick Creamy Dip

When you need something good...and fast!

8-oz. pkg. cream cheese, softened
2 c. sour cream

1 envelope dry onion
   soup mix

Mix and serve with crackers.

Victorian Blackberry Punch

A pretty, rich color and delicious berry flavor.

1-1/2 c. sugar
3 c. water
3 c. strong tea
juice of 6 lemons
juice of 4 oranges

2 c. grape juice
1 c. pineapple juice
1 c. blackberry juice
1 c. raspberry juice
5 c. ice water

Dissolve sugar in 3 cups water in saucepan. Boil for 5 minutes. Combine tea, syrup, fruit juices, and ice water in a large container. Pour over ice mold into punch bowl. Garnish with lemon and orange slices. You may want to try this sometime with cranberry juice instead of blackberry juice.

Yield: 20 cups.

Pacific Northwest Appetizer

One of our favorite appetizers for Christmas parties.

8-oz. pkg. cream cheese
1/2 lb. crab or fresh shrimp, shelled (small ones)
1 jar of cocktail sauce
assortment of crackers

Take the cream cheese out one hour before serving. Spoon and smooth into a small serving bowl and put shrimp or crab on top of the cream cheese. Pour cocktail sauce over crab and cream cheese. Serve with an assortment of crackers.

Ranch Snack Mix

A crunchy treat for your bunch who loves to munch.

1 envelope ranch-style
   dressing mix
1 c. canola oil
1 t. dill weed
1 t. garlic powder

2 c. mini shredded
   wheat squares
2 c. mini pretzels
1 c. blanched peanuts
   or mixed nuts
1 c. shelled
   sunflower seeds

Combine dressing mix, oil and seasonings; mix well. Mix all other ingredients in a bowl; pour oil mixture over all and stir to coat well. Spread on a baking pan and place in 250 degree oven for 15 to 20 minutes. Stir once in the middle of baking.

Makes 6 cups. Store in airtight containers.

Grease the lip of your cream pitcher with butter at that holiday gathering...it will prevent gravy from dripping all over your favorite tablecloth, and it will be easier clean up for you!

Baked Mushrooms

Serve with assorted crackers and sourdough rounds.

3/4 lb. mushrooms,
   finely chopped
2 T. butter
1 T. sherry

8-oz. pkg. cream cheese,
   softened
2 T. onion, finely chopped

Sauté mushrooms in butter until lightly golden brown. Add sherry and let evaporate over low heat. Turn off the burner and stir in cream cheese and onion. Blend until well mixed. Transfer mixture to oiled or buttered baking dish. ☆ (If you have one, use an au gratin or oval baker.) Bake at 350 degrees for 25 minutes. Allow to cool and garnish with parsley to serve.

Syllabub

A very old-fashioned, deliciously creamy drink.

1/2 c. milk
1/2 c. sugar
2-1/2 c. fresh apple cider
1 t. vanilla extract

speck of salt
2 c. heavy cream
freshly grated
   nutmeg, for garnish

In a large mixer bowl, combine the milk, sugar, cider, vanilla and salt. In another bowl, whip the cream until stiff; fold the whipped cream into the cider mixture, then whisk until the syllabub is frothy and completely combined. (It can be stored in the refrigerator at this point; whisk again to recombine before serving.) Serve in punch cups and garnish with grated nutmeg.

Cheese Bread

An easy favorite for brunch, snack time or any time.

1-1/4 c. milk
3-3/4 c. biscuit mix
1-1/4 c. Cheddar cheese,
    shredded

1 egg, beaten
1 t. dry mustard
poppy seeds

Preheat oven to 325 degrees. Mix all ingredients just to blend. Beat vigorously for one minute. Pour into greased loaf pan. Sprinkle top with poppy seeds. Bake for 55 to 60 minutes. Cool slightly.

Citrus Mimosa

Makes the champagne go a little further!

1 c. prepared strawberry
    daiquiri mix
6-oz. can frozen orange juice
    concentrate, thawed
6 oz. cold water
3/4 c. fresh grapefruit
    juice

1/3 c. frozen lemonade
    concentrate, thawed
3 T. frozen limeade
    concentrate, thawed
1 bottle champagne,
    chilled
thin orange slices, halved

Combine prepared daiquiri mix, orange juice concentrate, water, grapefruit juice, lemonade and limeade concentrate in a pitcher or bowl. Stir until well combined. Cover and chill. To serve, pour the chilled juice mixture into eight ice-filled glasses, filling each glass half-full. Pour an equal amount of the chilled champagne into each glass. Garnish with orange slice halves. Makes 8 (6-ounce) servings.

Note: For a nonalcoholic drink, substitute chilled carbonated water for the champagne.

Mushroom Logs

Delicious tidbits.

2 8-oz. cans crescent
   dinner rolls
8-oz. pkg. cream cheese,
   softened
2 4-oz. cans mushroom
   pieces, drained & chopped
   (or 16 oz. fresh)

1 t. seasoned salt
1 bunch scallions, chopped
1 T. Worcestershire sauce
1 t. lemon pepper
1 egg, beaten
2 T. poppy seeds (optional)

Separate dough into four rectangles, pressing seams together.
Combine cream cheese with mushrooms, salt, scallions,
Worcestershire sauce and lemon pepper. Spread evenly over
rectangles. Roll into logs, starting with long side of rectangle.
Pinch seams. Brush with egg, sprinkle with poppy seeds. Cut into
one-inch pieces. Place on ungreased cookie sheet, seam side down.
Bake at 375 degrees for 10 to 12 minutes.

Delightful Decoration

Dip baby pine cones
into copper paint.
When dry,
scatter them
among the
hors d'oeuvres
on your
buffet table.

Avocado-Tomato Salsa

Fresh and spicy...delicious with tortilla chips or toasted pita bread!

1/2 avocado,
   diced into 1/4" pieces
2 medium tomatoes,
   diced into 1/4" pieces
1 green onion, minced
1 T. cilantro, chopped

1 jalapeño pepper,
   seeded and minced
2 t. lemon juice
1/4 t. ground cumin
1/4 t. olive oil
1/2 t. garlic salt

Mix all ingredients lightly and serve at once. It may be kept up to 2 hours before serving, but as it sets longer, more juice accumulates. If you like a thinner salsa, it may be made a day ahead of time.

Old-Fashioned, Homemade Eggnog

It's the real thing and there is a difference!

6 eggs
1/2 c. sugar
1/4 t. salt
3 c. milk

1 t. vanilla
1/2 t. ground nutmeg
1 c. heavy cream

In pan, beat eggs, sugar and salt. Stir in milk. Cook, stirring, about 15 minutes or until mixture coats spoon. Remove from heat and stir in vanilla. Chill overnight. Just before serving, whip cream to soft peaks. Whisk into egg mixture in a gentle folding motion. Serve with extra nutmeg or a dusting of cinnamon.

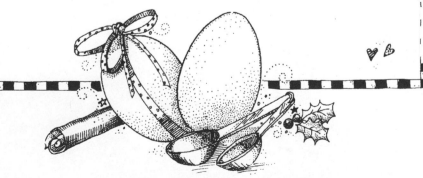

36

Yuletide Crab Puffs

This recipe can be made ahead of time, filling just before serving. Puffs can be frozen for later use.

1 lb. flaked crab meat
2/3 c. celery, chopped
1/2 c. onion, finely chopped
4 hard-boiled eggs,
    finely chopped

2 T. chili sauce
salt and pepper to taste
1 T. fresh parsley, minced
1-1/2 or 2 c. mayonnaise

Mix above ingredients together until well blended, adding enough mayonnaise to make the mixture bind together. Refrigerate this mixture until shortly before serving. You will use this mixture to fill the puffs (recipe below). Do not fill puffs very far in advance of serving; the result will be soggy puffs.

Yield: 4 cups of filling.

Puffs:

1 c. water
1/2 c. butter (1 stick)

1 c. flour, sifted
4 eggs

Bring water to a boil; add butter. Stir this mixture until butter is melted. Add flour, stirring until dough forms a ball. Cool dough mixture. Beat eggs in a separate bowl, until very thick and lemon-colored. Stir eggs into cooled dough and mix thoroughly. Drop onto a baking sheet by teaspoonfuls. Bake for 15 minutes at 400 degrees. Cool puffs on rack. Slice and fill with crab mixture just before serving.

A bayberry candle
burned to the socket brings luck
to the house, food to the larder,
and gold to the pocket.

Tomie de Paola

scrumptious
sideboard

Make-Ahead Mashed Potatoes

What's the first thing to get cold while the dinner table's being set? Of course...the mashed potatoes! These recipes will never let this happen again! There are two versions to this easy, quick way to make mashed potatoes guaranteed to arrive at your holiday table still warm.

Potatoes Version #1

8 potatoes, peeled and sliced
8 oz. cream cheese, softened
1/2 c. sour cream
1/2 t. onion powder
salt to taste
paprika

In a saucepan, combine potatoes and enough water to cover. Bring to a boil. Reduce heat and cook 20 minutes or until potatoes are tender. Drain. Mash potatoes, gradually adding cream cheese, sour cream, salt, and onion powder until fluffy. Spoon into a casserole dish and sprinkle with paprika. Bake at 350 degrees for 30 minutes or until thoroughly heated. Or, if made ahead, cover and refrigerate overnight. When ready to serve, bake the casserole uncovered at 350 degrees for 45 minutes, or until thoroughly heated.

Potatoes Version #2

6 c. (2 lbs.) potatoes, peeled, quartered
1/2 c. mayonnaise or salad dressing
8 oz. cream cheese, softened
1/2 or 3/4 t. salt
1/4 t. white pepper
1/2 t. onion powder
paprika

In a saucepan, combine potatoes and enough water to cover. Bring to a boil. Reduce heat and cook 20 minutes or until potatoes are tender. Drain. Mash potatoes until fluffy, gradually adding mayonnaise, cream cheese, salt, pepper, and onion powder. Spoon into a casserole dish and sprinkle with paprika. Bake at 350 degrees for 30 minutes, or until thoroughly heated. Or cover and refrigerate overnight. When ready to serve, bake the casserole uncovered at 350 degrees for 45 minutes, or until thoroughly heated.

Jalapeño Cornbread

Really good on New Year's Day with Hoppin' John and cabbage.

1 stick butter, unsalted
1/2 c. onion, chopped
1 clove garlic, minced
1 roasted red pepper, peeled,
   seeded and chopped
1 or 2 fresh jalapeños,
   finely chopped
1 c. whole kernel corn
1-1/2 c. yellow cornmeal

1 c. flour
1/2 c. sugar
1 T. baking powder
1 t. salt
1-1/2 c. buttermilk
2 eggs, slightly beaten
1 c. Monterey Jack cheese,
   shredded

Preheat oven to 350 degrees. Melt butter in a 10-inch cast-iron skillet. Sauté onion, garlic, red pepper, jalapeños, and corn kernels until tender, about 5 minutes. In a large bowl, sift together cornmeal, flour, sugar, baking powder and salt. Stir in buttermilk and eggs. Add sautéed mixture, stir until incorporated. Add cheese and stir. Pour batter back into the skillet; bake for 30 to 35 minutes, until golden brown or edges are firm to the touch. Let the cornbread sit for 20 to 30 minutes before cutting into wedges.

Icy Lemonade Waldorf Salad

A little different twist on the Waldorf classic.

4 navel oranges, peeled,
   cut in sections
4 red delicious apples,
   cut in wedges
1 c. celery, sliced or diced

13-1/2 oz. can pineapple
   chunks, drained
6-oz. can frozen
   lemonade concentrate,
   slightly thawed

Combine all ingredients. Pour lemonade over salad and chill.

Roberta's Carrot Ring

Something a little different and very colorful!

2 c. carrots, cooked, mashed
1 c. evaporated milk
1/2 c. margarine
1/8 t. cayenne pepper
2 eggs, beaten

1 c. saltines, crushed
3/4 c. cheese, grated
1 t. salt
1/4 c. onion, diced

Combine all ingredients and put into a greased bundt pan. Bake at 350 degrees for 40 to 45 minutes.

Cheesy Lima & Tomato Casserole

Try this one with spinach instead of lima beans. Also very delicious!

1/4 c. onions, minced
2 T. butter
4 c. canned tomatoes, crushed
2 10-oz. pkgs. frozen lima
    beans, cooked and drained

1 t. salt
2 t. chili powder
3 T. flour
1/4 c. water
2 c. Cheddar cheese, grated

Cook onion in butter. Add tomatoes, limas, salt and chili powder. Simmer uncovered for 10 minutes. Blend flour into water to make a paste. Stir into vegetables and cook over low heat to thicken. Put into a casserole dish and top with cheese. Bake at 350 degrees for 20 minutes.

An old Yugoslavian custom is to bake bread on Christmas Eve for family and friends. What is so special about this bread? After it's baked, a large gold coin is inserted inside, and when it's served, it's anyone's guess who will receive that special piece. Children especially enjoy this old-fashioned tradition for the holidays.

Hearty Ground Sirloin Soup

A stick-to-your-ribs sort of soup.

1/2 lb. ground sirloin
4 or 5 cans (14-1/2 oz. each)
   chicken broth
1/2 c. onion, diced
2 c. water
4 carrots, cut in chunks
4 celery stalks, sliced

4 potatoes, diced
45-oz. can pinto beans
14-oz. can kidney beans
28-oz. can crushed tomatoes
1/2 T. dried basil and parsley
white pepper
8 oz. vermicelli

Sauté ground sirloin until meat is brown. Add chicken broth. Combine remaining ingredients except vermicelli and cook until vegetables are almost done (about 1/2 hour). Bring to a boil, add vermicelli noodles, cover and simmer 10 more minutes.

Serves 8.

Whipped Fruit Butter

Perfectly yummy on toast, muffins, pancakes and waffles!

1/2 c. whipped butter
1-1/2 t. half and half
1 T. orange juice
1 t. orange peel, grated

1 T. sugar
1/2 t. cinnamon
1/4 c. golden raisins, chopped

Beat butter and half and half at high speed until fluffy. Add the remaining ingredients and beat again.

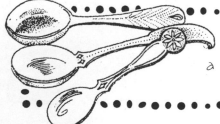

Arrange your silverware for
a buffet dinner by nesting it in
a pretty bread basket lined with linen
and topped with a bow.

Onion Mushroom Soup

Rich in fresh, creamery butter and topped with melted cheese.

4 large onions, peeled
   and cut into rings
8 oz. fresh mushrooms, sliced
   (can be canned)
6 c. rich beef stock
12-oz. can chicken stock

1 stick butter
dash Worcestershire sauce
flour
1/4 c. red wine (optional)
slices of French or Italian bread
slices of mozzarella cheese

In a large Dutch oven, sauté the onions in half the butter until tender. Remove to a side bowl. Add the remaining butter and mushrooms and sauté. Take out the mushrooms and add to the onions. Mix one or 2 tablespoons of flour into the butter until pasty. Add some stock and whisk until all blended. Add remaining stock, wine, Worcestershire sauce, and boil. Reduce to a simmer and add the onions and mushrooms. Add salt and pepper to taste. When ready to serve, put soup in oven-proof bowls, add a slice of bread, and top with cheese. Put in a 350 degree oven until cheese melts.

Serves 8 to 10.

43

Deluxe French Toast

It looks as good as any breakfast served at an inn.

4 whole eggs
2 egg whites
1 pint milk
1-1/2 t. vanilla
2 T. sugar

1 loaf Jewish braided egg bread
   cut into 1/2" thick slices
1 T. butter
1 t. vegetable oil
Topping: powdered sugar,
   maple syrup or fruit butter

Beat eggs, egg whites, milk, vanilla, and sugar together with whisk. Poke holes in each slice of bread and soak in egg mixture. Melt butter with vegetable oil in a large skillet over medium heat. Grill bread until golden brown. Serve sprinkled with powdered sugar, drizzled with syrup or topped with butter.

Holiday Wassail

This is great if someone in the house has a cold because it's full of Vitamin C. If you're ever snowbound for a day, brew up a pot. At the end of the day discard the oranges and save the rest in a pitcher in the refrigerator. Then just microwave a mug before bedtime or when you come in from the outdoors.

1 c. orange juice
2 juicy oranges, pitted, sliced in half
   and studded with whole cloves
4 c. apple juice

4 c. cranberry juice cocktail
sprinkle of cinnamon
sprinkle of allspice

In a crock pot or in a large pot on the stove, stir the above ingredients together. Heat until boiling, or leave in crock pot on low all day. The crock pot smells wonderful in the house as it simmers, and you don't have to keep reheating it...just ladle a cupful whenever you'd like. Serve in a mug with a cinnamon stick or a candy cane. Drink while hot.

Hot Fruit Salad

What an easy, warm, Christmasy way to serve fruit.

20-oz. can chunky applesauce
15-oz. can pineapple
  chunks, drained
15-oz. can sliced
  peaches, drained
15-oz. can apricot
  halves, drained

1 small can mandarin
  oranges, drained
1 large can cherry pie filling
1/2 c. brown sugar
1 t. cinnamon

Mix all together in a 13"x9" pan. Bake one hour at 350 degrees.

Triple Corn Stuffing

A really different stuffing to try...goes great with turkey or chicken.

1/2 c. butter
1-1/2 c. celery, chopped
1 c. onion, minced
2 T. parsley, minced
2 t. poultry seasoning
1/4 c. water or chicken broth

16-oz. pkg. cornbread-style
  stuffing mix
1 c. popped popcorn, finely
  ground (grind in blender or
  food processor until crumbled)
16-oz. can creamed corn

In a large skillet, melt butter over low heat; sauté celery and onion until clear. Add water, parsley, and seasoning; mix well. Cook on low for 2 minutes. Mix in stuffing mix and ground popcorn, blending well. Add creamed corn and mix until thoroughly moistened. You may stuff a medium-sized turkey with this or bake at 350 degrees for about 30 minutes in a buttered casserole dish.

Instead of using bowls or dishes to serve your holiday dips, use red and green bell peppers. Easy to clean up and very festive.

Christmas Cranberry Rolls

Double or triple this recipe. These freeze well and you'll have them in the freezer for gatherings from Thanksgiving to New Year's.

1 c. milk	2 eggs, beaten
4 T. butter or margarine	1/2 t. ginger
1/4 c. sugar	1 t. cinnamon
1/2 t. salt	4-1/2 or 5 c. flour
2 T. yeast	1/2 c. cranberries, chopped
1/4 c. warm water	

Heat milk to the boiling point. While it is warming up, add butter, sugar, and salt to dissolve. Remove from heat and cool to lukewarm. Dissolve yeast in warm water in bowl. Add cooled milk, eggs, ginger and cinnamon to the yeast mixture. Stir in flour until it is a very sticky dough. Knead 3 to 4 minutes, adding flour when needed. In another small bowl, add some flour to the chopped cranberries so that they are coated in flour. Knead the cranberries into the dough. Remove dough from the bowl; set aside. Clean the bowl and lightly coat with oil. Return dough to the oiled bowl and cover with a cloth. Let it rise until it doubles in size. Turn dough out onto the counter and roll out to 1/2-inch thick. Cut with a circle cookie cutter, or roll into small balls and put three in each cup of a muffin tin to make cloverleaf rolls. Let rise until doubled in size. Bake at 350 degrees for 25 minutes or until golden brown. Rub butter on tops when they come out of the oven.

Each batch makes about 2 dozen rolls.

Eggnog Bread (for large capacity bread machine)

Leftover eggnog is great in pancake batter, French toast, muffins, quick breads, or cookie recipes...any place that milk could go.

1-1/8 c. eggnog (non-alcoholic)	2 t. active dry yeast
3 T. canola oil	1/2 c. raisins (if your machine
1/2 t. salt	has a "beep" for adding
3 c. bread flour	ingredients, add at the "beep")

Place items in your machine as the manufacturer suggests. Bake on "sweet" or "white" setting. You should not use a delay timer because the eggnog could spoil. Watch the dough after about 5 minutes of kneading time and adjust flour or liquid by one table-spoonful at a time to form a ball in your pan.

Yield: one loaf.

Tangerine-Cranberry Relish

To serve with your Christmas ham or turkey.

1 lb. fresh or frozen cranberries	2 c. seedless raisins or
4 tangerines	nuts, coarsely chopped
1-1/2 or 2 c. sugar	

Wash cranberries (do not thaw frozen berries) and put through the medium blade of food chopper. Wash tangerines and remove peel. Put the peel through a food chopper. Remove seeds from tangerines and cut sections into small pieces. Combine cranberries, tangerine peel and pieces and sugar; stir until sugar is dissolved. Add raisins or nuts, blend well and turn into glass jars. Cover and refrigerate. Relish will keep for several weeks.

Makes 2-1/2 pints.

Mushrooms Florentine

Savory and elegant...a big hit!

16-oz. pkg. fresh
   mushrooms
10-oz. pkg. frozen
   spinach, chopped
2 T. butter or margarine
1/4 to 1/2 t. garlic powder

1/2 c. bread crumbs
   or cracker crumbs
1/2 c. Parmesan cheese
salt and pepper to taste
dash of nutmeg

Wash mushrooms and remove stems. Set stems aside. Melt one tablespoon of butter or margarine. Dip mushroom caps into melted butter or margarine and place into large baking dish with opening facing up. Cook frozen chopped spinach according to package directions. Drain and set aside. Chop mushroom stems and sauté in one tablespoon of melted butter or margarine. Remove from heat. Add garlic powder, salt and pepper, nutmeg, bread crumbs, and 1/4 cup of the Parmesan cheese. Mix well. Fill each mushroom cap with about one tablespoon of spinach mixture. Sprinkle remaining Parmesan cheese on top of filled mushroom caps. Bake at 350 degrees for about 20 to 25 minutes. Serve while hot.

Serves 10 to 12 people.

This might be the first year
the reindeer spill carrot "crumbs" onto the front lawn.
Surprise your kids by putting shredded carrots
all over the lawn.

Festive Ham and Potato Salad

Looks great with radish roses, a wedge of hard-cooked egg, and cherry tomatoes.

1/3 c. sour cream	2-1/2 c. (approx. 12 oz.)
3 T. green onions, minced	cooked ham, cubed
4 t. white vinegar	1-1/2 c. cooked potatoes, diced
1/4 t. salt (optional)	1/2 c. celery, chopped
1/8 t. pepper	1 hard-boiled egg, chopped
1/2 t. dill weed (optional)	1 c. cottage cheese
	(small curd preferred)

In a small bowl combine sour cream, green onions, white vinegar, salt, pepper, and dill weed. Set aside. In a large bowl combine ham, potatoes, celery, egg, and cottage cheese. Fold sour cream mixture into ham mixture. Cover and chill for at least 2 hours to allow time for flavors to blend. Serve on a bed of lettuce.

At the office Christmas party, have everyone bring some canned food items so they can be contributed to the food bank.

Cheddar Cheese Biscuits

Easy drop biscuits with just the right amount of spice.

2 c. self-rising flour
1/4 t. cayenne pepper
1/2 t. dry mustard
6 or 8 T. butter-flavored
   shortening

1 c. sharp or medium Cheddar
   cheese, grated
1 c. milk
melted butter
garlic powder to taste

Mix flour, cayenne pepper and dry mustard in a large bowl. Cut in shortening. Fold in grated cheese. Add enough milk to make a stiff dough that will drop from a spoon. Drop dough onto a greased pan by the tablespoon. Brush tops with melted butter and sprinkle with garlic powder. Bake in 450 degree oven for 12 to 15 minutes until nicely browned.

Hot Cranberry Butter

Try this with pancakes on a cold winter's morning. Yum!

2 c. cranberries, fresh or frozen
1 c. granulated sugar
1/2 c. water

1/4 c. brown sugar
1/4 c. butter

Combine cranberries, granulated sugar and water in saucepan. Heat to boiling, stirring until sugar dissolves. Boil until berries pop (about 5 minutes). Add brown sugar and butter. Heat until dissolved. Serve hot with French toast, waffles, or pancakes.

Cranberry Broccoli Salad

Colorful, crunchy and refreshing.

1-1/4 c. fresh cranberries, halved
2 c. broccoli flowerets
4 c. cabbage, shredded
1 c. walnuts, coarsely chopped
1/2 c. raisins
1 small onion, finely minced

8 slices bacon, cooked
   and crumbled
1 c. mayonnaise
1/3 c. sugar
2 T. cider vinegar

In a large bowl combine cranberries, broccoli, cabbage, walnuts, raisins, onion, and bacon. Combine remaining ingredients and pour over cranberry mixture. Toss well. Cover and refrigerate for up to 24 hours.

Yield: 6 to 8 servings.

Christmas Tree Pull-Apart Rolls

Very yummy...so festive with dinner!

36 unbaked rolls, frozen
2 t. parsley, dried and crumbled
garlic salt to taste
1/4 c. Romano cheese
2 T. butter, melted

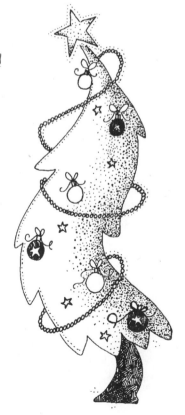

Arrange rolls on a cookie sheet in a Christmas tree pattern. As they thaw out and rise, the "balls" come together. Bake the rolls according to instructions. When you remove them from the oven, they will be formed into a single piece. Transfer to a platter and brush with melted butter. Sprinkle with garlic salt, Romano cheese and parsley. Serve immediately.

Savory Brunch Bread

Delicious with your favorite omelet and freshly squeezed orange juice.

1/4 c. Parmesan cheese, grated
3 T. sesame seeds
1/2 t. dried basil, crushed
1 pkg. 24 unbaked
   dinner rolls, frozen

1/4 c. butter or
   margarine, melted
2 t. real bacon bits

Grease a 10-inch fluted tube pan. In small bowl combine Parmesan cheese, sesame seeds and basil. Add 1/3 mix to pan and turn to coat sides. Place 10 frozen rolls in pan and drizzle with half of the butter. Sprinkle with half of the remaining cheese mix and with bacon bits. Add remaining rolls. Drizzle with remaining butter and sprinkle with remaining cheese. Cover; let rolls thaw and rise overnight (12 to 24 hours) in the refrigerator. The next day, let stand at room temperature 30 minutes. Bake uncovered at 350 degrees for 20 minutes. Cover with foil and bake 10 to 15 minutes more until golden brown. Remove from pan to wire rack and serve warm.

Serves 12.

Sweet Potato Bake

Here's a favorite dish with a crunchy topping.

40-oz. can sweet
   potatoes, drained
1/2 c. sugar

1/2 stick margarine, softened
2 eggs
1 c. evaporated milk

Topping:

1 c. coconut
1 c. corn flakes, crushed

1/2 stick margarine

Beat potatoes, sugar, margarine, eggs and milk with electric mixer until well beaten. Put into baking dish and bake at 375 degrees for about 20 minutes. Add topping and bake at 375 degrees for 15 more minutes.

Oatmeal Muffins

Serve warm with hot coffee and crisp bacon.

1 c. quick oats
1 c. whole wheat flour
1-1/2 t. baking powder
1/2 t. baking soda
1/2 t. salt
1/2 c. brown sugar, packed

1/2 c. oil
1 large egg, beaten
1 c. milk or buttermilk
1/2 c. raisins
1/2 c. nuts, broken

In medium bowl stir oats, whole wheat flour, baking powder, soda, salt and brown sugar, blending well. Stir in oil, egg and milk just until blended. Stir in raisins and broken nuts. Bake in a 12-muffin tin at 350 degrees for 25 minutes.

Eggnog Cherry Muffins

Make an assortment of muffins and put them out on Christmas morning.

2-1/2 c. flour
3/4 c. sugar
1 T. baking powder
1 t. salt
1 egg, beaten

1-1/2 c. eggnog
1/3 c. oil
1/2 c. walnuts, chopped
1/2 c. maraschino
    cherries, chopped

Mix dry ingredients together. Combine egg, eggnog and oil and gently blend into dry ingredients. Stir in walnuts and cherries. Spoon into muffin tins and bake at 350 degrees for 20 minutes, or until tested done. Makes 12 large muffins.

At your neighborhood Christmas party, invite the local high school choir to come caroling. What a crowd-pleaser!

Baked Broccoli

You can add sliced water chestnuts if you want a little more crunch. Very good!

1/2 c. celery, chopped
1/2 c. onion, chopped
2 T. butter
10-oz. pkg. frozen
   broccoli, chopped
2 c. rice, cooked
10-3/4 oz. can cream of
   chicken soup

1/2 c. milk
8-oz. jar prepared
   American cheese sauce
1/4 c. bread crumbs,
   buttered or seasoned

Sauté celery and onion in butter. Add broccoli and stir until broken up and slightly cooked. Mix together remaining ingredients in a separate bowl. Add to broccoli mixture. Put in sprayed casserole dish. Cover with buttered crumbs. Bake at 350 degrees for 20 to 30 minutes.

Corn Casserole

Try topping with buttered bread crumbs before baking.

1/2 c. margarine, melted
2 eggs, beaten
1/2 c. corn meal
1/2 t. onion salt
1 c. sour cream

1 can creamed corn
1 c. grated Jack or
   Cheddar cheese
4-oz. can diced chilies
   or green pepper

Mix all ingredients together. Bake in an 8-inch square baking pan at 350 degrees for 50 to 60 minutes.

Salmon Chowder

Serve with thick, buttered slices of sourdough bread.

3/4 c. onion, chopped
1/2 c. celery
1 clove garlic, minced
   (or 1 t. garlic powder)
3 T. butter or margarine
2 c. potatoes, diced
2 cans or 4 c. chicken broth
1 t. salt

1 t. pepper
1 t. dill weed
2 carrots, diced
2 cans of cooked
   salmon, flaked
13-oz. can evaporated milk
1 can creamed corn
1/2 lb. Cheddar cheese, grated

Sauté onion, celery and garlic in butter. Add potatoes, chicken broth, seasonings and carrots. Cover and simmer 20 minutes. Add salmon and liquid, evaporated milk and corn. Continue cooking until heated through. Serve with cheese sprinkled on top.

Sweet Potato Soufflé

As Uncle Jack used to say, "It's out of this world!"

2 lbs. sweet potatoes,
   cooked and mashed
1/4 c. margarine, melted
1/4 c. brown sugar
1/2 c. milk

salt
1 t. cinnamon
1/4 t. mace
2 eggs, beaten

Mix above ingredients well and transfer to a buttered casserole dish.

Topping:
2 T. butter
1/3 c. flour

1/4 c. brown sugar
1 c. walnuts, chopped

Mix together topping ingredients and crumble over sweet potato mixture. Bake at 350 degrees for 30 minutes.

Apples And Sweet Potatoes

A good combination with your ham or turkey dinner.

4 c. sweet potatoes,
   thinly sliced
4 c. tart apples, thinly sliced
1 T. instant minced onions
   (or to taste)

1 t. salt
3/4 c. pure maple syrup
3/4 c. apple cider
1/2 c. butter, melted

Arrange layers of sweet potatoes and apples in buttered 2-quart casserole dish. Mix remaining ingredients and pour over all. Cover and bake at 350 degrees for one hour or until vegetables are tender.

Creamy Mushroom Barley Soup

Thick, hearty and healthy.

2 T. butter
1 small onion, chopped
1 lb. mushrooms, sliced
1 c. carrots, sliced thinly
1/2 c. quick-cook barley
1 c. chicken broth

1 c. water
2 c. milk
1 c. half and half
1 T. flour
1 t. salt
1/4 t. pepper

Sauté vegetables in butter and cook about 6 minutes. Add barley, broth and water. Simmer covered for 15 minutes, or until barley is tender. Add remaining ingredients and cook, stirring, until it comes to a boil and is thickened. Purée two cups of the soup in a food processor. Stir back into the soup pot and heat through.

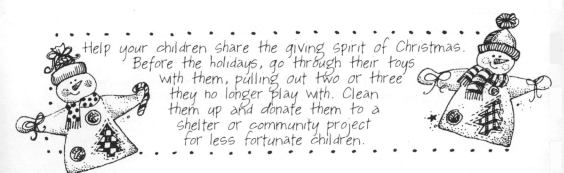

Help your children share the giving spirit of Christmas. Before the holidays, go through their toys with them, pulling out two or three they no longer play with. Clean them up and donate them to a shelter or community project for less fortunate children.

Peanut Vegetable Soup

A delicious taste...you may add diced cooked chicken
to this recipe.

2 to 3 T. butter or vegetable oil
1/2 c. carrots, chopped
1/2 c. zucchini, chopped
1/2 c. red or green bell
   pepper, chopped
1/2 c. red cabbage, shredded

1/2 c. onion, chopped
3 T. flour
5 c. chicken broth
1 c. creamy peanut butter
1 c. light cream
salt and pepper to taste

Sauté vegetables in butter or oil until crisp-tender. Add flour
and stir until smooth. Add broth and bring to boil. Stir in peanut
butter. Reduce heat and simmer about 15 minutes. Remove and stir
in cream. Garnish with chopped peanuts.

Cornbread Dressing

If you like it very moist, add 1/2 cup of cooked grits.

2 c. celery, chopped
2 c. onions, chopped
1/3 or 1/2 c. butter
1 pan baked cornbread,
   crumbled

2 eggs, beaten
1 t. poultry seasoning
2 T. dried parsley
4 c. cooled chicken broth
pepper

Combine all ingredients together and toss lightly. Bake in a
greased baking dish at 350 degrees for 45 minutes.
Chopped walnuts and sliced water chestnuts
may be added.

Easy Artichoke Rice Salad

A quick version of a great salad. Try adding 1/2 cup cooked wild rice to this recipe.

1 pkg. chicken-flavored
   rice and noodles
2 small jars marinated
   artichoke hearts, sliced
   (reserve juice)
1 green pepper, diced

3 celery stalks, diced
1 t. curry
1/2 c. mayonnaise (fat-free)
12-oz. bottle of green stuffed
   olives, chopped
black pepper to taste

Prepare the rice and noodles mixture according to the instructions on the box. Combine with the marinated artichoke hearts, juice, green pepper, celery, and curry. Mix mayonnaise and olives together and blend into rice mixture. Season to taste and chill.

Cranberry Buttermilk Muffins

You can make these muffins with 1/4 cup of applesauce and half the oil.

1 large egg
1 c. buttermilk
1/3 c. oil
1 c. flour
   (white or whole wheat)
1-1/2 t. baking powder
1/2 t. baking soda
1/2 t. salt
1 c. quick oats
1/2 c. brown sugar, packed
1/2 c. nuts, chopped
1/2 c. dried sweetened
   cranberries, chopped

Beat egg, buttermilk and oil with whisk. Add remaining ingredients and stir just until blended. Spoon into 12 muffin tins prepared with non-stick spray. Bake at 350 degrees for about 25 minutes, testing with a toothpick.

Mother's Celery Cornbread Dressing

Be sure to toss ingredients lightly for a nice, fluffy dressing.

14-oz. pkg. cornbread
   dressing mix
14-oz. pkg. herb dressing mix
8" square pan of baked
   cornbread, broken into pieces
2 eggs, beaten
1 small jar mushroom
   slices, drained

2 c. diced celery
packet of chicken broth mix
poultry seasoning to taste
1/2 can water chestnuts,
   drained and sliced
1/3 c. butter, melted
turkey broth

Mix all ingredients together lightly, using enough turkey broth to flavor dressing without making it soggy. Lightly spoon into pan and bake uncovered at 350 degrees for one hour.

Mother's Vegetable Casserole

Healthy and good...
what mother wouldn't love it?

1 envelope broth powder,
   prepared with water
1 pkg. seasoned wild rice
1 pkg. French-cut
   green beans, frozen
16-oz. can fat-free
   cream of mushroom soup

1/2 c. fat-free mayonnaise
1/2 c. water chestnuts, sliced
2 T. pimentos, diced
2 T. onion, chopped
10 almonds, toasted and
   crushed
1-1/2 c. cooked chicken, cubed

Cook seasoned wild rice in 2-1/3 cup broth just until done. Don't add oil. Cook green beans; do not drain. Combine rice and green beans with soup, mayonnaise, water chestnuts, pimentos, onion, almonds, and chicken. Add some broth if dry. Add pepper to taste. Bake at 350 degrees for about 30 minutes, or until heated through.

Mom's Mashed Potato Rolls

A favorite old family recipe.

1 c. mashed potatoes
1/2 c. sugar
2 eggs
1 pkg. yeast
1/2 c. lukewarm water

1 c. milk, scalded
6 c. flour
2/3 c. shortening
1-1/2 t. salt

Cream potatoes and sugar. Add eggs and beat. Add remaining ingredients and knead. Dough will be soft. Place in a large bowl. Cover and let rise in a warm place until doubled. Punch down. Brush with one teaspoon melted butter. Cover and refrigerate overnight. Punch down in the morning. Shape into rolls. Let rise again in a warm place. Bake at 350 degrees until golden.

Squash Casserole

A good side for turkey or ham. You may want to top with bread crumbs before baking.

5 or 6 yellow squash, cooked
    and drained (save water)
1 pkg. cornbread stuffing
2 celery stalks, chopped
1/2 small onion, chopped
2 T. butter
2 large eggs, beaten

1 c. mild Cheddar
    cheese, grated
10-3/4 oz. can cream
    of mushroom soup
1 c. chicken broth
1/4 c. walnuts, chopped

Mash squash with potato masher and combine with stuffing mix, adding remaining squash water if too dry. Sauté celery and onion in butter until tender. Stir into squash mixture along with eggs and grated cheese. Stir in mushroom soup. If dry, add a little more water. Add broth and walnuts. Pour into a greased 8-inch square baking dish. Bake at 350 degrees for 30 minutes.

Serves 6.

Green Beans with Mushroom Sauce

Top with sliced water chestnuts, peanuts or French fried onion rings to garnish.

4 oz. mushrooms, sliced
   (fresh or canned)
1 small onion, diced
1/4 c. butter
1/4 c. flour
3 c. milk
6 oz. processed cheese, diced

1/8 t. hot pepper sauce
2 t. soy sauce
pepper to taste
1 t. seasoned salt
   flavor enhancer
2 pkgs. French-cut green
   beans, cooked

Sauté mushrooms and onion in butter for about 3 minutes. Add flour and small amount of milk, stirring so flour will not lump. Add remaining milk, stirring as for white sauce. Add remaining ingredients except green beans. Stir sauce into green beans. Heat thoroughly.

Leave a Santa hat
by the tree and tell the children,
"Oh, my, Santa dropped his hat!"
Save it for next year and
leave it out so
Santa can come back
to retrieve his hat.

Pecan Sweet Potatoes

A new twist on an old favorite...the pecans and pineapple make it special!

3 large yams, cooked
1/2 c. pineapple juice
1/3 c. pecans, chopped
3 T. butter or margarine

1/4 to 1/3 c. brown sugar
1 t. cinnamon
dash of salt
mini marshmallows (optional)

Mash cooked yams with pineapple juice. Toast pecans in a hot buttered skillet. Add brown sugar and a little more pineapple juice, cinnamon and salt. Mix well. Spread in 8-inch casserole dish. Sprinkle mini marshmallows on top, if you like. Bake at 350 degrees for 20 minutes, or until heated through.

Strawberry Cream Cheese Mold

For fun, try different holiday molds; garnish with frosted grapes as well as strawberries.

3-oz. pkg. strawberry gelatin
3/4 c. hot water
1 pkg. strawberries, thawed
1 small can crushed
    pineapple, drained
3-oz. pkg. lemon gelatin

1 c. hot water
8-oz. pkg. cream cheese,
    room temperature
1 c. whipping cream, whipped
1/2 c. pecans, chopped
fresh strawberries as garnish

Mix strawberry gelatin, hot water, strawberries, and pineapple. Put in a mold to set. Mix lemon gelatin with hot water and chill until partially set. Mix cheese with a little cream to soften. Add cheese and nuts and whipped cream to gelatin. Mix, pour over first layer, and chill. Fresh strawberries dipped in powdered sugar may be used in center of mold.

Spanish Rice

Keep the hot sauce handy!

1 green pepper
1/4 c. onion, chopped
1 lb. sirloin, ground
chili powder to taste
16-oz. can vegetable juice
32-oz. can crushed tomatoes

1 c. water
1 c. rice
1 c. beef or vegetable broth
1 c. sharp Cheddar
    cheese, grated

Sauté green pepper, onion and ground sirloin in a frying pan with the chili powder until meat is brown and vegetables are tender. Add vegetable juice, crushed tomatoes, water, rice and broth; stir. If thick, add a little more water and broth. Cook covered about 20 minutes, or until rice is tender. A little white pepper may also be added. Cover with cheese and serve in a covered casserole dish.

Sweet Stewed Cabbage

Delicious with tender country ribs or pork chops.

1 T. oil
6-oz. can pineapple juice
1/4 c. brown sugar
1 T. white sugar

1 head red cabbage
pinch of salt
pinch of garlic powder
juice of 2 fresh lemons

In a big pan put oil, pineapple juice and both sugars. Cook until caramelized. Stir with fork. Add cabbage. Stew about 30 minutes with lid on until tender. Add a pinch of salt and garlic powder and juice of fresh lemons. Adjust sugar and lemon juice to taste.

> Splurge on a big bolt of gold metallic florist's ribbon. Wind it around your Christmas tree for a lovely garland.

Hush Puppies

Serve with fried chicken and green beans for a great taste of the South.

3/4 c. corn meal
1/3 c. self-rising flour
2 T. sugar

1 t. baking powder
1/2 t. salt
approx. 1/4 c. milk

Mix and wet the above ingredients with enough milk to drop from a spoon into hot oil. Fry until golden brown on each side. Diced sweet onion may be added to this recipe.

Judy's Country Cornbread

Go ahead and serve it in the skillet!

3/4 c. corn meal
1 c. flour
1 t. salt
1 T. baking powder
1/4 c. sugar
1 c. milk
2 large eggs
1/4 c. oil

In a medium bowl, stir corn meal, flour, salt, baking powder and sugar. Add milk, eggs and oil. Stir with fork until just blended. For a country look, bake and serve in a 9-inch iron skillet. (Spray with non-stick spray first.) Bake at 400 degrees for 30 minutes.

Long, Long Ago

Winds through the olive trees
Softly did blow
'Round little Bethlehem
Long, long ago.

Sheep on the hillside lay
Whiter than snow.
Shepherds were watching them
Long, long ago.

Then from the midnight sky
Angels bent low
Singing their songs of joy
Long, long ago.

*

Soft in a manger bed
Cradled so low,
Christ came to Bethlehem
Long, long ago.

Anonymous

Bountiful Banquet

Orange Chicken

Just as delicious with the skin removed. Try this one with brown rice, too!

2-1/2 or 3-lb. pkg. select chicken
   pieces (breasts, thighs
   and drumsticks)
salt and pepper to taste
medium white onion, sliced

1 c. orange juice
1/3 c. honey
1 T. soy sauce
2 T. flour
2-1/2 c. cooked white rice

Wash and dry chicken pieces; salt and pepper to taste. Make a bed of sliced white onions in a large baking pan. Lay chicken pieces on onions. Make a sauce of orange juice, honey and soy sauce whisked together. Pour over chicken and bake at 325 degrees for one hour or until done. Remove chicken and place pan on stove burner. Add flour and cook until you have a slightly thickened sauce. Serve over steamed white rice.

Triple Cranberry Sauce

This is pretty served in a footed glass compote.

1 c. frozen cranberry juice
   concentrate
1/3 c. sugar
12-oz. pkg. fresh or frozen
   cranberries, rinsed, drained

1/2 c. dried cranberries
   (about 2 oz.)
3 T. orange marmalade
2 T. fresh orange juice
2 t. orange peel, minced
1/4 t. allspice, ground

Combine cranberry juice concentrate, sugar and cranberries in heavy medium saucepan. Bring to boil over high heat, stirring often until berries begin to soften and fresh berries begin to pop, about 7 minutes. Remove from heat and stir in orange marmalade, orange juice, orange peel, and allspice. Cool completely. Cover and chill until cold, about 2 hours. Can be made 3 days ahead. Keep refrigerated.

Makes about 2-1/2 cups.

Phyllo Roll with Cranberry Sauce

The ham, mushrooms, and melted cheese go very well with tangy cranberry sauce.

1/3 c. celery, chopped
1/3 c. green pepper, chopped
1/4 c. green onion, sliced
1-1/2 t. cooking oil
1-1/2 c. fully cooked ham
   (7 oz.), diced
4-oz. can mushrooms
   stems and pieces, drained
1/2 c. Cheddar or Monterey Jack
   cheese, shredded

1 T. flour
1/4 t. pepper
1/3 c. butter or
   margarine, melted
1 T. fine dry bread crumbs
8 sheets frozen phyllo dough
   (18"x14" rectangles), thawed
1 egg white, beaten

In a large saucepan, cook the celery, green pepper and onion in hot oil until tender. Remove from heat. Drain well. Stir in ham, mushrooms, cheese, flour and pepper. Lightly brush one sheet of phyllo with melted butter and sprinkle with 1/2 teaspoon of bread crumbs. Top with remaining sheets of phyllo, brushing each sheet and sprinkling with crumbs. Brush top sheet with egg white. Mound ham mixture on the phyllo dough stack, parallel to and about 3 inches from one of the long edges. Fold the 3-inch ends of dough over the edges of the ham mixture. Roll up from the long side (like rolling a jelly roll). Using a sharp knife, make shallow cuts about an inch apart in diagonal criss-cross fashion across the top. Place the roll in a 13"x9" baking pan. Brush with more of the butter. Cover and chill, up to 24 hours. (Now is also a convenient time to freeze it!) To serve, uncover roll. Bake in a 400 degree oven for 25 to 30 minutes or until golden and heated through. Slice and serve warm with cranberry sauce.

Makes 4 servings. Doubles easily.

Busy Day Casserole

Easy and satisfying on a cold winter day!

1-1/2 lbs. ground beef or turkey; browned, drained and rinsed

2 medium onions, chopped and mixed in with meat

1 large green pepper, cut into thin strips

1-lb. box of rigatoni, elbow, or shell macaroni

2 15-oz. cans of tomatoes chopped or crushed

clove of garlic, minced (or 1/2 t. garlic powder)

black pepper

chili powder to taste

8-oz. block of sharp (or mild) Cheddar cheese, shredded

Optional: 1 can mushrooms, any size, added to the tomato sauce

In a Dutch oven, brown meat with onions and green pepper. Drain off the fat and rinse lightly. Cook the noodles and set aside. Spray a casserole dish lightly with vegetable spray. Set aside. Put tomatoes in a bowl, add the garlic, a sprinkle of black pepper, and a sprinkle of chili powder, according to taste. In the casserole dish, place enough sauce to cover the bottom, some meat, noodles, sauce, and half the cheese. Repeat layers, ending with the cheese. Bake at 350 degrees for 45 minutes, covered. Uncover the last 5 minutes. Serve with rolls and a salad, and you have a quick meal. This can be made ahead and frozen. Pop it in about an hour before dinner. It's great for the night of the "game," late practice, or PTA meeting. A good dish to fall back on around the holidays, when you don't feel like cooking a big meal.

Chicken in Sour Cream

This crowd-pleaser actually melts in your mouth.

2 c. sour cream
1/4 c. fresh lemon juice
4 t. Worcestershire sauce
2 t. celery salt (a must)
2 t. paprika

1 clove garlic, pressed
1 t. pepper
10 to 12 boneless chicken breasts
16-oz. box Italian bread crumbs
1 stick butter or margarine

Combine sour cream, lemon juice, Worcestershire sauce, celery salt, paprika, garlic, and pepper in a large deep bowl with lid. Add chicken breasts and coat the chicken well. Allow to marinate in the sour cream mixture overnight in the refrigerator, covered. When ready to cook, remove pieces of chicken from the sour cream sauce and roll in the bread crumbs. Arrange in a single layer in a 13"x9" pan sprayed with vegetable spray and drizzle the butter over the chicken. Bake uncovered at 350 degrees for 45 minutes or until done. This is great served with a green salad, wild rice and rolls. Excellent for picnics served cold, too!

Baked Jumbo Shrimp

Christmas dinner doesn't have to be the traditional turkey meal...especially for shrimp-lovers!

4 T. butter
2 T. good, imported olive oil
2 T. vegetable oil
2 T. fresh parsley, snipped

4 T. fresh lemon juice
2 lbs. jumbo shrimp or scampi,
   peeled and butterflied

Preheat oven to 450 degrees. Put butter in a flat 13"x9" baking dish. Place in preheated oven and heat until butter is foamy. Remove dish from oven. Add the remaining ingredients to the butter and stir. Add shrimp, turning to coat with butter mixture. Arrange shrimp. Bake 6 to 10 minutes depending on the size of the shrimp. Remove from oven and serve immediately. This goes well with rice of some kind, a green salad, and broccoli with cheese sauce.

Christmas Breakfast Strata

A great Christmas breakfast. This can be made late
Christmas Eve and popped in the oven on Christmas morning.

1 loaf French bread, sliced
   and torn into pieces
4 c. Cheddar and Monterey
   Jack cheese, shredded
2 rolls breakfast sausage, cooked
1 can green chilies, diced
1 small can black olives, sliced

mushrooms, sliced
6 to 8 eggs
4 c. milk
2 T. oregano
1 t. salt
1 t. dry mustard
1 t. powdered onion

Butter a 13"x9" and 8"x8" baking pan and place torn and buttered bread in the bottom of the pans. Sprinkle cheeses over the bread. Sprinkle the cooked sausage, diced green chilies, olives, and mushrooms over the cheese. Beat the eggs and add milk, oregano, salt, dry mustard, and powdered onion. Pour liquid over the mixture and sprinkle with any remaining cheese. Bake at 350 degrees for one hour or until a knife blade comes out clean. Serve with sour cream and salsa. Serve English muffins and fresh fruit alongside.

Cranberry-Orange Glazed Cornish Hens

This makes a wonderfully delicious holiday dinner for two.

2 fresh or frozen
   Rock Cornish game hens
2 T. butter, melted
1/4 c. whole cranberry sauce
2 T. orange marmalade

1 T. lemon juice
1 t. minced dried onion
1 t. cornstarch
1/2 c. mandarin orange
   sections, drained

Thaw hens, if frozen. Rinse hens and pat dry. Coat inside and outside of hens with melted butter; sprinkle with salt and pepper. Place hens, breast side up, on a rack in a shallow roasting pan. Insert a meat thermometer. Cover loosely with foil. Roast in 375 degree oven for 30 minutes. Uncover and roast about one hour more or until meat thermometer registers 185 degrees. Meanwhile, for sauce, in a one-quart saucepan, combine cranberry sauce, orange marmalade, lemon juice, minced onion, and cornstarch. Cook and stir until thick and bubbly. Cook and stir for 2 more minutes. Remove from heat; stir in orange sections. Brush over hens several times during last 20 minutes of roasting.

Thinking of giving a pet kitten or puppy this Christmas?
Be sure it will be wanted and cared for!
Include a good book on pet care along
with recommended food from your local pet store.
Make sure the new "baby" has had its shots.
Give it a good start in life with its new owner.

Holiday Tropical Ham

A sweet, crusty glazed ham for your main event.

1 fully cooked
    boneless whole ham
15-oz. can sliced peaches
8-oz. can crushed pineapple
2 T. cornstarch
1/2 t. cinnamon
dash ground cloves

1/3 c. frozen orange juice
    concentrate, thawed
1/2 c. whole
    maraschino cherries
1/4 c. golden raisins
handful of toasted pecans
    (optional)

Score ham in a diamond pattern, cutting only 1/4-inch deep. Drain peaches and pineapple; reserve syrups. Combine cornstarch and spices with syrup, orange juice concentrate and one cup water in a large saucepan. Cook and stir until bubbly, then cool while ham bakes. Bake ham according to weight. The last 30 minutes of baking, arrange peaches and pineapple on top of ham, spoon some sauce mixture on top and continue baking. Add cherries, nuts, and raisins to remaining sauce and reheat. Serve with the ham.

Serves 10 to 15.

Raisin Sauce For Christmas Ham

Delicious served with sweet potatoes and applesauce.

3/4 c. raisins
1 c. water
4 or 5 whole cloves
3/4 c. brown sugar, not packed
1 t. cornstarch

1/4 t. salt
1/4 t. pepper
1 T. butter or margarine
1 T. lemon juice
1/4 t. Worcestershire sauce

Cover raisins with water, add cloves and simmer for 10 minutes. Mix sugar, cornstarch, salt, and pepper, and add to raisin mixture. Stir until thickened over low heat. Add butter, lemon juice, and Worcestershire sauce, stirring until thoroughly combined. Simmer a few minutes. Baste ham with mixture while baking.

Christmas Luncheon Crabmeat Bisque

Or make a shrimp bisque by replacing crab with 1-1/2 cups cooked, deveined shrimp.

6 T. butter
4 T. green pepper, finely chopped
4 T. onion, finely chopped
1 scallion, chopped
2 T. parsley, chopped
1-1/2 c. fresh mushrooms, sliced
2 T. flour
1 c. milk

1 t. salt
1/8 t. white pepper
dash of hot pepper sauce
1-1/2 c. half and half
1-1/2 c. cooked crabmeat,
   canned or fresh
3 T. dry sherry

Heat 4 tablespoons butter or margarine in a skillet. Add green pepper, onion, scallion, parsley, and mushrooms, and sauté until soft, about 5 minutes. In saucepan, heat remaining 2 tablespoons margarine or butter and stir in flour. Add milk and cook, stirring until thickened and smooth. Stir in salt, pepper, and hot pepper sauce. Add sautéed vegetables and half and half. Bring to a boil, stirring; reduce heat. Add crabmeat, simmer uncovered for 5 minutes. Stir in sherry just prior to serving.

Serves 4.

Warm Country Gingerbread Waffles

Can be served with brown sugar, powdered sugar, hot maple syrup, or berries.

2 c. flour
1/2 t. salt
1/2 t. ground ginger
1 t. cinnamon
1 c. molasses

1/2 c. butter
1-1/2 t. baking soda
1 c. cream or sour milk
1 egg

Sift all dry ingredients. Heat molasses and butter until butter melts. Remove from heat and beat in baking soda. Add milk and egg, then add sifted flour mixture. Bake batter in waffle iron, making sure that iron is not too hot.

Makes approximately 6 to 8 waffles, depending on size.

Mel's Christmas Morning Casserole

A whole breakfast, baked and ready to go!

6 eggs, slightly beaten
1/2 c. Cheddar
   cheese, shredded
1/2 c. mozzarella
   cheese, shredded
1 t. dry mustard
1 T. parsley flakes

1 T. dried onion flakes
1 t. oregano
1 lb. ground Italian sausage,
   browned and drained
1 c. biscuit mix
2 c. milk

On Christmas Eve, mix all ingredients and pour into a lightly greased lasagna pan. Cover and refrigerate overnight. On Christmas morning, while everyone is opening gifts, pop the pan into a 350 degree oven and bake for one hour. By the time everyone is ready for breakfast, it will be hot and ready to eat. To save fat, sodium, and calories, you can substitute fat-free egg substitute for eggs, low-fat biscuit mix for regular, omit up to 1/4 cup cheese, substitute low-fat skim or 2% milk, and rinse cooked Italian sausage in hot water, draining well before adding.

Makes 10 to 12 servings.

Honeyed Canadian Bacon

This really rounds out a special breakfast. It truly is a great addition to any hearty country meal.

1/2 c. raisins
1-3/4 c. cider
1/3 c. honey
1 T. cornstarch

3/4 t. dry mustard
6 slices Canadian bacon
6 slices pineapple

Combine raisins and cider and simmer for 10 minutes. Add honey. Combine cornstarch and mustard and stir into cider mixture and cook another 3 minutes, stirring constantly. Bake bacon in shallow baking pan in 350 degree oven until done, usually 30 minutes if slices are 1/2-inch thick; adjust time accordingly. During the last 15 minutes of baking, remove from the oven and place a pineapple slice on each piece of Canadian bacon. Pour sauce over all and return to the oven.

Serves 6.

Day-After Turkey Muffin Cups

Taste like little turkey pot pies.

1/4 c. celery, finely chopped
3 T. green pepper, chopped
1/4 c. onion, chopped
1 T. margarine
2 c. cooked turkey, chopped

2 T. mayonnaise
1/2 t. salt
1/2 c. almonds, chopped
1 can refrigerator biscuits
  (can of 10)

Sauté celery, pepper, onion, and margarine in skillet until tender. Add turkey, mayonnaise, salt, and almonds. Mix thoroughly. Place each biscuit in a greased muffin cup. Press the biscuit dough evenly into cups. Spoon turkey mixture evenly into 10 cups. Bake at 350 degrees for 15 to 20 minutes, just until biscuits are lightly browned.

Ham 'n Turkey Casserole

Here's what to do with all those leftovers!

3 ribs of celery, chopped
1/4 c. butter or margarine
1/4 c. flour
1/2 t. salt
1 c. milk or chicken broth
1 c. light cream
2 T. sherry
3-oz. can mushrooms
2 t. minced onion
  (or dried flakes)

2 t. prepared mustard
1 c. sour cream
2 c. cooked medium noodles
  (4 oz. dry)
1-1/2 c. cooked turkey, cubed
1-1/2 c. cooked ham, cubed
1/4 c. slivered almonds,
  toasted

Sauté the celery in butter until crisp-tender. Stir in flour and salt. Add milk or broth (broth preferred) and cream. Cook mixture until thick and bubbly, stirring constantly. Stir in sherry, then add all other ingredients, except the almonds. Place mixture in a 2-quart casserole dish and top with almonds. Bake 25 minutes at 325 degrees. May take slightly longer to cook if turkey, ham, and other ingredients are cold when added to the broth and cream mixture.

Serves 6.

Cheese-Topped Crab Casserole

For a double seafood-lover's treat, you can add shrimp to this recipe.

2 T. butter or margarine
1 small jar of mushrooms
2 c. milk
2 T. flour
1/4 c. white wine

16 oz. fresh, frozen
  or canned crabmeat
1/2 c. bread crumbs
1/2 to 1 c. Cheddar
  cheese, grated

Sauté mushrooms in butter (cook slowly). Add flour alternately with milk to make white sauce. Let thicken. Add wine and simmer 2 to 3 minutes. Put crabmeat in a casserole dish. (If using frozen crabmeat, allow to thaw first.) Cover with mushroom and wine sauce. Top with bread crumbs and cheese. Bake at 350 degrees for 40 minutes. Serve over noodles or rice.

Serves 4.

Sausage Stuffed Acorn Squash

Try this recipe on anyone who says they don't like squash!

1 lb. pork sausage meat
3 medium acorn squash
1/4 c. butter or margarine
    (melted)
salt to taste

10-oz. pkg. frozen mixed
    vegetables (partially thawed)
1 c. Cheddar cheese, cubed
    (about 1/4 lb.)

Preheat oven to 350 degrees. In 10-inch skillet over medium high heat, cook sausage until browned, about 10 minutes, breaking it apart with fork. Drain off and discard fat. Cut squash in half lengthwise and remove seeds. Place halves, cut side up, in roasting pan. Brush insides with some melted butter and sprinkle with salt. In medium bowl, combine sausage, mixed vegetables, cheese cubes and salt to taste. Divide mixture among squash halves and brush tops with remaining butter. Cover pan tightly with foil or lid and bake in preheated oven for 1-1/2 hours or until squash is fork tender.

Serves 6.

Turkey and Dressing Bake

An easy way to relive the joys of Christmas dinner.

8-oz. pkg. herb-seasoned
    stuffing mix
2 T. onion, finely chopped
10-3/4 oz. can condensed
    cream of mushroom soup,
    divided in half

2 c. turkey or chicken stock
2 eggs (well beaten)
2-1/2 c. turkey meat,
    cooked & diced
1/2 c. milk
2 T. chopped pimento

Preheat oven to 350 degrees. In a bowl, toss stuffing mix with onion, 1/2 can mushroom soup, the turkey or chicken stock and eggs. Spread mixture in an oblong baking pan and top with diced turkey. Mix the remaining 1/2 can of mushroom soup with milk and pimento and pour over turkey and dressing. Cover pan with foil and bake in preheated oven for 45 minutes or until set.

Serves 6 to 8.

Dozen Egg Corn Casserole

Feed the gang well before a day of shopping!

12 eggs, beaten
2 17-oz. cans corn,
   cream-style
4 c. (1 lb.) sharp Cheddar
   cheese, shredded

2 4-oz. cans green chilies,
   drained and chopped
1 T. salt
1 T. Worcestershire sauce
1/2 t. pepper

Preheat oven to 325 degrees. In large bowl combine all ingredients and beat until well mixed. Pour into 13"x9" baking dish. This can be prepared ahead. Cover and refrigerate up to 24 hours. Bake one hour and 15 minutes, or until firm to touch.

Makes 6 to 8 servings.

Resolve to make double quantities of meals on the weekends after Thanksgiving. Make up one dish to serve and one to freeze, eliminating the hassle of cooking during the hustle and bustle of the holidays at least two days each week. Rediscover your crock pot for at least one other meal during each week, and assign one meal to someone else in the family. Even children can make sandwiches and soup, and most love to be a part of making a meal happen. The remaining evening meal can be a "wild card" night...order in pizza and salad or make a just-for-fun meal out of leftovers. Instant no-stress cooking!

Cranberry Chicken

Quick and easy...remove the skin from the chicken for a lighter version of the glaze.

chicken fryer pieces, cut up
(as many as your family needs)

1 bottle French dressing
1 can whole cranberry sauce
1 envelope dry onion soup mix

Place chicken in baking dish and top with remaining ingredients. Bake at 350 degrees for one hour, keeping the baking dish covered for the first half. Makes a delicious glaze.

Shrimp Sauté

If you love garlic, add more to this savory dish.

1 c. uncooked orzo (tiny pasta)
1 T. plus 1 t. olive oil
2 cloves garlic, peeled
    and minced
20 large fresh or frozen shrimp,
    peeled and deveined

salt and pepper to taste
1/4 c. parsley
juice and zest of 1 lemon
1 c. dry wine
5 T. butter

Cook orzo al dente (until still a bit chewy), drain and toss with one tablespoon olive oil. Salt and pepper to taste. Add remaining oil to frying pan. Cook garlic one minute and add shrimp, salt, pepper and 2 tablespoons parsley. Cook 3 to 4 minutes; turn and cook 3 minutes longer. Add lemon juice and wine to skillet. Bring to boil for 2 minutes. Add remaining parsley. Stir in butter and lemon zest. Pour over shrimp and serve on platter of orzo.

Hanging racks

Baked French Toast

Serve hot from the oven with little sausage links
and maple syrup.

3 T. butter, melted
1-1/2 c. milk
3 eggs
2 T. powdered sugar
1 t. vanilla

1/2 t. ground cinnamon
1/8 t. ground nutmeg
6 large slices of good
   quality bread

Heat oven to 475 degrees. Drizzle melted butter on a jelly roll pan. Whisk together milk, egg, powdered sugar, vanilla, cinnamon and nutmeg. Dip both sides of the bread into this mixture. Place in prepared pan. Pour any remaining milk mixture over bread. Let it stand 20 minutes. Turn over bread. Bake at 475 degrees for 15 minutes or until puffed and golden brown.

Cranberry Tea

When you want a   great winter warm-up.

7 regular tea bags
1 gal. water, boiling
1 t. whole cloves
3 cinnamon sticks
6-oz. box cranberry
   gelatin

1/2 c. sugar
6-oz. can frozen
   orange juice, thawed
1 qt. cranberry juice
1 qt. apple juice

In a two-gallon container, steep tea bags in one gallon of boiling water for six minutes. Remove bags. Add cloves and cinnamon and simmer for 30 minutes. Remove. Dissolve sugar and gelatin. Add rest of ingredients and simmer for 30 minutes. Serve hot.

Corned Beef & Cabbage

Very tasty...try this recipe in your crock pot and let it simmer all day!

2 lbs. corned beef brisket
1/2 c. diced onion
1 bay leaf

1 head of cabbage,
   cut into wedges
1 lb. of carrots

Place all ingredients in a Dutch oven. Cover brisket with water, bring to a slow boil; then reduce heat and simmer over low heat for 2 hours.

David's Chicken Pieces

The way kids love to eat chicken...serve with honey mustard dressing for dipping!

4 boneless, skinless chicken
   breast halves, cut into pieces
2 T. Italian salad dressing mix

1-1/2 to 2 c. biscuit mix
2 T. oil

Mix together biscuit mix and salad dressing mix. Put in a brown bag. Shake chicken pieces in bag to coat. Brown in a medium-hot skillet in a small amount of oil. Drain on a paper towel.

Chicken Breasts Chablis

Delicious and tender...add mushrooms to the sauce, if you like!

1/4 c. flour	2 T. cornstarch
1 t. salt	1 T. Dijon mustard
1/4 t. pepper	1-1/2 c. milk
4 large chicken breasts,	1 t. salt
boneless and skinless	3/4 c. Chablis or
2 T. butter	other white wine
2 T. oil	1/4 t. tarragon
3 T. butter	

Preheat oven to 350 degrees. Mix flour, salt and pepper; dredge chicken and sauté in 2 tablespoons of butter and 2 tablespoons of olive oil until brown. Arrange in baking dish. To make the sauce, melt 3 tablespoons butter in a saucepan. Whisk in mustard and corn-starch. Cook until it comes to a boil (keep whisking) and add milk, salt, wine and tarragon. Cook until it thickens while stirring. Cook one more minute, then pour over chicken. Cover and bake 45 minutes to an hour. Serve over hot cooked noodles, rice, or mashed potatoes.

Creamed Chicken Delight

No need for gravy, the mushroom sauce is great on mashed potatoes or rice.

12-oz. jar or pkg.	1 can cream
chipped beef, sliced	of mushroom
4 whole skinless, boneless	soup (low-fat)
chicken breasts	1-1/2 c. light
2 c. mushrooms, sliced	sour cream

Add water to a small saucepan and bring chipped beef to a boil; drain to remove salt. Put in bottom of a baking pan. Arrange chicken breasts on top of beef. In a bowl, whisk mushroom soup and sour cream together. Spread over chicken. Sprinkle with mushrooms. Bake uncovered at 275 degrees for 2-1/2 hours. Serve with mashed potatoes.

Sorghum Fried Chicken

A sweet, tender flavor...great with scalloped potatoes and a crisp, green salad.

4 chicken breasts,
　skin removed
1 c. flour
1 t. salt

pepper to taste
1 t. dried oregano, crushed
1/2 c. sorghum molasses
1 or 1-1/2 T. water

Mix dry ingredients. Mix water and sorghum. Dip chicken in sorghum, then in flour mixture. Dip again in sorghum and then in flour mixture. Fry in hot oil until just brown on each side. Place on a rack in a baking pan and bake at 350 degrees for 30 minutes.

Serves 4.

Cheesy Mexican Pizza Quiche

For brunch or dinner...serve salsa on the side.

2 T. cornmeal
refrigerated crescent rolls,
　sliced into 16 pieces

1 c. colby or Monterey Jack
　cheese, grated
4 eggs
1 c. cottage cheese
6-oz. can artichoke
　hearts, drained
2 oz. diced pimentos
4-oz. can chilies

Coat a 13"x9" pan with non-stick spray. Sprinkle with cornmeal. Slice crescent rolls into 16 slices. Lay in pan. Cover with grated cheese. Beat eggs with cottage cheese. Stir in artichoke, pimentos and chilies. Pour over crescent rolls. Bake at 375 degrees for 30 minutes.

Hot Chicken Salad

This dish is also very good made with leftover turkey.

1 c. cooked chicken, diced
1-1/2 c. celery, chopped fine
1 c. toasted almonds, sliced
1/8 t. salt (optional)
1/4 c. onion, grated
1 c. green pepper, chopped
1 c. mayonnaise
   (can be fat-free)

1/4 c. pimento, chopped
1/4 c. lemon juice
10-3/4 oz. can cream of
   chicken soup, undiluted
2 eggs, hard-boiled, chopped
2 c. Cheddar cheese, grated
crushed potato chips

Combine all ingredients in a 5-quart shallow casserole dish except chips and cheese. Mix well. Top with cheese. Bake at 350 degrees for 30 minutes. Place potato chips on top and bake another 10 minutes.

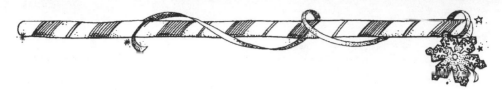

Family Favorite Carrot Cake

Also makes great cupcakes.

2 c. flour
2 c. sugar
2 t. soda
2 t. cinnamon
1/2 t. salt
3 large eggs, lightly beaten
3/4 c. oil
3/4 c. buttermilk

2 t. vanilla
8 oz. crushed pineapple,
    drained
2 c. raw carrots, grated
1 c. coconut, flaked
1 c. walnuts, chopped
1 c. chocolate chips (optional)

Frosting:

1/4 c. butter, softened
4 oz. cream cheese, softened

1 t. vanilla
2 c. powdered sugar

Mix together flour, sugar, soda, cinnamon and salt. Combine eggs, oil, buttermilk and vanilla and add to dry ingredients. Stir in pineapple, carrots, coconut, walnuts and chocolate chips. Pour into sprayed 13"x9" pan. Bake at 350 degrees for 45 to 55 minutes. Mix together frosting ingredients and frost when cool.

Cherry Cream Pie

Serve a scoop of vanilla ice cream on the side.

1 lb. graham cracker
    crumbs
3/4 c. butter, melted
2 T. sugar
2 pkgs. whipped topping mix

1-1/2 c. powdered sugar
8-oz. pkg. cream cheese,
    softened
2 cans cherry pie filling

Mix graham cracker crumbs, butter, and sugar. Press into a 13"x9" pan. Bake at 350 degrees for 8 minutes. Mix topping according to package directions. Add powdered sugar and cream cheese. Pour into crust and top with cherry pie filling. Chill for 30 to 35 minutes.

Mom's Candy Apple Walnut Pie

The red hots add the spice.

6 c. thinly sliced cooking apples
    (Jonathan, Rome or Granny
    Smith), with or without peel
2/3 c. walnuts, chopped

1/2 c. cinnamon red hot candies
1/3 c. plus 2 T. sugar
1/3 c. all-purpose flour
2 deep-dish pie crusts, frozen

In a large bowl, toss together apples, walnuts, cinnamon candies, 1/3 cup sugar and flour. Pour into one frozen pie crust. Break and crumble second frozen crust into very small pieces; toss with remaining 2 tablespoons sugar. Sprinkle over apples. Bake in preheated 375 degree oven on a preheated baking sheet 55 to 60 minutes or until candies melt and bubble up through the crumbled crust. Cool completely before serving.

Makes 8 servings.

Snowballs with Cranberry Sauce

This steamed cake has a very smooth, moist texture.

1 box white 2-layer cake mix,
    prepared with listed ingredients
1 c. sugar

1 c. water
2 c. cranberries
1 T. cornstarch

Prepare cake mix according to package directions. Pour into 8 greased custard cups. Cover each with foil. Put on a rack in a large kettle with about one inch of hot water. Cover and steam about 25 minutes. Turn out of cups and serve hot with cranberry sauce.

Cranberry Sauce:

Cook sugar and water about 5 minutes. Add cranberries and cook until skins burst. Mix cornstarch with a little cold water and stir into cranberry mixture. Bring to a boil.

Makes 8 servings.

Grandma Essie Hill's Blackberry Cobbler

This recipe dates back to 1910...it's just as tasty today as it must have been 'way back then!

5 c. fresh blackberries	4 t. baking powder
1-1/4 c. sugar	1/2 t. salt
2 T. butter	1/2 t. cream of tartar
3-1/2 T. flour, sifted	1/2 c. butter
2 c. flour, sifted	1/2 c. milk
2 T. sugar	

Toss blackberries with sugar and pour them into a well-buttered 1-1/2 quart oblong baking dish. Sprinkle with 3-1/2 tablespoons flour and dot with butter; set aside. Into a bowl, sift remaining flour and sugar, baking powder, salt, and cream of tartar. Cut in 1/2 cup butter until the mixture resembles coarse meal. With a fork, stir in milk and form the mixture into a ball. Roll the dough out 1/4-inch thick on a floured board. Cover the blackberries with the dough and trim the edges. Cut a vent in the center of the dough and sprinkle the top generously with sugar. Bake the cobbler in a 400 degree oven for 40 minutes or until the crust is golden. Serve warm with cream.

Don't forget to take photographs of the everyday joys of the holidays. Take pictures of family members occupied with the tasks they enjoy...Dad stringing the outside lights, the kids rolling out cookie dough, Mom wrapping presents, cozy pictures of the family just curling up by the fire. Pictures bring back the fondest memories.

Aunt Hara's Butter Pecan Buns

Sticky, sweet and oh so good!

2 loaves (2-lb. pkg.)
   frozen sweet dough
   (or your favorite recipe)
1/2 c. light corn syrup
2 T. water
4 T. butter

2 c. butterscotch chips
1 c. pecans, chopped
1/4 c. butter
2/3 c. brown sugar,
   firmly packed
Optional: raisins to taste

Defrost sweet dough as package directs or let homemade dough rise. In skillet, combine corn syrup, water and butter. Bring to a boil over medium heat, stirring constantly. Remove from heat and stir in butterscotch bits until melted. Spread mixture over bottom of two ungreased 9"x9"x2" pans. Sprinkle with chopped nuts. Roll out half the dough on a floured surface to a rectangle 12"x9". Brush with melted butter, sprinkle with half the brown sugar and raisins, if used. Roll each rectangle from the 9-inch side as for jelly roll. Seal edges. Cut each roll into nine one-inch slices and place over butterscotch mixture in pans. Repeat for remaining dough. Let rise until puffy. Bake at 350 degrees for 30 to 35 minutes. Remove from oven, loosen edge. Invert onto a rack placed over wax paper to catch drips. Quickly spoon up drips and put back on top of buns. Makes 18 buns.

Take time out to help a child
make a Christmas present
for a family member.

Banana Cake

Serve with whipped topping and a dash of cinnamon.

2/3 c. butter, melted
2 c. sugar
2 eggs, beaten
1 t. vanilla
1 c. buttermilk

3 ripe bananas
1 t. baking soda
1 t. baking powder
2-1/2 c. flour

Cream butter and sugar. Add eggs and vanilla. Blend buttermilk and bananas. Combine dry ingredients. Alternate milk mix and dry ingredients, blending into sugar mixture. Bake at 350 degrees in a greased and floured 13"x9" pan for 45 minutes.

Al's Favorite Cake

This is the cake we make for Al's birthday...by special request!

1 box 2-layer white cake mix
3/4 c. water
3/4 c. oil
4 large eggs
1 large pkg. chocolate
     pudding mix
3/4 c. sugar
3/4 c. milk

2 T. flour
2 large egg yolks
2 T. butter, softened
1 banana, mashed
1/2 c. walnuts, chopped
whipped cream or prepared
     whipped topping
1/2 c. coconut

Mix cake mix, water, oil, 4 eggs and chocolate pudding mix together. Beat well. Pour into sprayed 13"x9" pan. Bake at 350 degrees for 37 minutes. Cool and slice horizontally. To make the filling, place sugar, milk, flour and egg yolks in a heavy pan. Whisk and cook until the consistency of pudding. Remove from heat. Add butter, mashed banana and chopped walnuts. Cool and fill cake. Frost cake with whipped cream and sprinkle with coconut. Keep chilled.

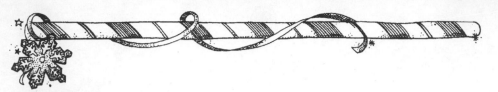

Pumpkin Pudding Cake

Very rich, and so easy!

3 eggs, beaten
1 c. sugar
1 t. cinnamon
1/2 t. salt
32-oz. can pumpkin
1/2 t. ginger (optional)
1/4 t. cloves

14-oz. can evaporated milk
1 box of 2-layer white or
   yellow cake mix
1 stick butter, melted
1 c. walnuts or pecans, chopped
whipped cream or ice cream

Mix eggs, sugar, cinnamon, salt, pumpkin, ginger, cloves and milk. Whisk until blended and pour into a greased or sprayed 13"x9" pan. Sprinkle one package cake mix over top. Drizzle melted butter over top. Sprinkle with chopped walnuts or pecans. Bake at 350 degrees for one hour. Serve with whipped cream or ice cream.

Scottish Shortbread

A very tender, rich cookie.

1 c. butter, softened
1 c. margarine, softened
1 c. powdered sugar

4 c. flour
1/2 t. baking powder
1/4 t. salt

Mix butter and margarine until creamy. Gradually add the sugar. Next add the dry ingredients. Turn the dough out onto counter and knead gently about 10 times. Shape into a rectangle on a large cookie sheet. Pierce at 2-inch intervals all along top of short-bread. Bake at 300 degrees (preheated) for one hour. Once properly browned, cut immediately into small rectangular shapes. Leave in pan to cool for 10 minutes, then transfer to a wire rack to cool completely. Store in an airtight container.

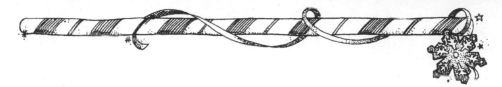

Amaretto Mousse Cheesecake

Scatter slivered almonds on top for a very pretty garnish.

2 c. graham cracker crumbs
1/2 c. butter, melted
1 envelope unflavored gelatin
1/2 c. cold water
3 8-oz. pkgs. cream
    cheese, softened

1-1/4 c. sugar
5-oz. can evaporated milk
1 t. lemon juice
1/3 cup Amaretto liqueur
1 t. vanilla
3/4 c. heavy cream, whipped

Combine the cracker crumbs with butter. Press into bottom and up sides of a 9-inch springform pan; chill. In a small saucepan, sprinkle gelatin over cold water. Let stand one minute. Stir over low heat until completely dissolved, about 3 minutes. Set aside. In a large bowl, beat cream cheese with sugar until fluffy, about two minutes. Gradually add the evaporated milk and lemon juice; beat at medium high speed until mixture is very fluffy, about two minutes. Gradually beat in gelatin mix, liqueur (or substitution) and vanilla. Fold in whipped cream. Pour into crust; chill 8 hours or overnight. Garnish with slivered almonds, maraschino cherries, etc. ♥ ▷

To omit Amaretto liqueur, increase water to 3/4 cup and add 1/2 teaspoon almond extract in addition to the vanilla.

93

Gingerbread Coffee Cake

Ten times better than any store-bought coffee cake!

1 c. water
1 c. molasses
1 t. baking soda
1 c. brown sugar
1 stick butter, softened
2 eggs, beaten

2 c. flour
1 T. baking powder
1 t. ground cinnamon
1/4 t. ground ginger
1/4 t. ground cloves

Preheat oven to 350 degrees. Grease a 13"x9" baking pan. Bring water and molasses to a boil. Stir in baking soda. Let cool. Beat sugar, butter, eggs in a bowl. In another bowl, combine flour, baking powder, cinnamon, ginger, cloves. Beat flour alternately with molasses, half at a time, into butter until well mixed. Pour into the prepared pan.

Topping:

1/3 c. flour
1/3 c. sugar
1/3 t. ground cinnamon

1/3 t. ground ginger
1/2 c. chopped walnuts
3 T. butter

Combine flour, sugar, cinnamon, ginger and walnuts in a bowl. Cut in butter with a pastry blender until mixture is coarsely crumbled. Sprinkle over gingerbread. Bake at 350 degrees for 40 minutes.

Glaze:

1 c. powdered sugar   1-1/2 T. milk   1/2 t. vanilla

Whisk sugar, milk and vanilla in a small bowl until soft enough to drip from a spoon. If needed, add more milk. Drizzle over top of lukewarm cake.

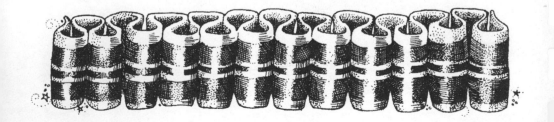

Lemon Mousse Mold

Surround with grapes, strawberries and kiwi slices. Very pretty!

1 envelope unflavored gelatin
1/2 c. lemon juice
3-oz. pkg. lemon gelatin
1 c. boiling water or
    pineapple juice
8 oz. cream cheese
2 c. milk

3-oz. pkg. instant
    lemon pudding
2 c. lemon yogurt
12-oz. tub of whipped topping
4 packets of sugar substitute
1/2 T. grated lemon rind
    (optional)

Sprinkle gelatin over lemon juice and set aside. In a small pan, dissolve lemon gelatin in boiling water. Now add unflavored gelatin mixture, dissolving well. Soften cream cheese in microwave and put in blender. Add hot gelatin mixture and blend until smooth. Let cool. In large bowl whisk or beat milk and pudding until well blended. Using a whisk, blend in the rest of ingredients. Pour into a sprayed bundt pan. Refrigerate overnight. Turn upside down onto a large platter to serve.

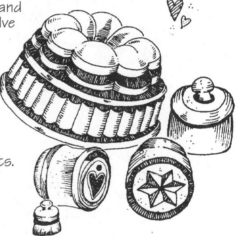

Every year, after the office Christmas party, purchase napkins, plates, toothpicks, candles, or anything storable for next year's gathering. This takes half of the pressure off for next year. Just label and store, and next year just worry about the food. Great for personal parties, too.

Brownie Trifle

This is a really easy recipe but it looks like you went to a lot of trouble. It must be made ahead, so it's a convenient, yet very elegant, end to a dinner party.

19.8-oz. pkg. fudge
   brownie mix
3.5-oz. pkg. instant
   chocolate mousse mix

8 1.4 oz. chocolate-covered
   toffee bars, crushed
12-oz. container frozen whipped
   topping, thawed

Prepare brownie mix and bake according to package directions in a 13"x9" pan. Let cool and crumble. Prepare chocolate mousse according to package directions, but do not chill. Place half of the crumbled brownies in the bottom of a 3-quart trifle dish. Top with half of the mousse, half of the crushed candy bars, and half of the whipped topping. Repeat layers with remaining ingredients, ending with the whipped topping. Garnish with chocolate curls if desired. Chill 8 hours.

Yield: 16 to 18 servings.

A great mom is worth her weight in brownie trifle!

Crunch Pie

The little ones will want to help with this one.

4 egg whites, beaten stiff
pinch of salt
1 c. sugar
1 t. vanilla

1 c. graham cracker crumbs
1/2 c. flaked coconut
1/2 c. pecans, chopped

Mix and pour all ingredients into a buttered pie pan. Bake at 350 degrees for 20 minutes. Serve with whipped cream.

Heavenly Black Forest Cake

Quick and easy, but it tastes like it took all day to make.

1 pkg. 2-layer devil's food
   cake mix
3 large eggs
1 can cherry pie filling

1 t. vanilla extract
1 T. real sour cream or
   vegetable oil
3/4 c. milk

Combine everything in a mixing bowl and beat together. If batter seems too thick, add a splash of water. Pour into a greased bundt or tube pan, or two layer pans. Bake at 350 degrees 25 minutes for layer pans, 45 to 55 minutes for bundt or tube pans. It is done when the top springs back when touched. Turn onto a pretty dish and sprinkle with powdered sugar, or ice as follows: Mix a box of vanilla instant pudding as directions indicate. Fold in a small container of whipped topping (the more topping, the lighter the frosting). Spread over the cake.

Decorating idea:

Take large marshmallows and cut in half with scissors. Put the cut side into some red sugar. Place a piece of citrus peel in the middle and make a flower. Add green spearmint leaves and decorate the top of the cake however you would like. Looks very festive! Refrigerate until serving.

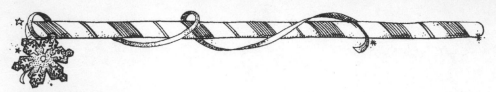

Peach Almond Pie

That yummy taste of the South.

4 c. fresh (or frozen) ripe peaches, sliced	1/4 c. flour
1/2 c. sugar	3/4 t. almond extract
	ready-made pie shell, unbaked

Gently stir ingredients into peaches. Put in unbaked pie shell.

Topping:

1/2 c. brown sugar	1/3 c. margarine
1/3 c. flour	1/3 c. almonds, slivered

Mix and sprinkle over peaches. Bake in a brown paper bag at 425 degrees for one hour.

Crème Brulée

A step up from pudding.
Serve with hazelnut coffee after dinner.

3/4 c. sugar	3 c. heavy cream
6 egg yolks	1/2 c. milk
1 T. vanilla extract	brown sugar

Mix sugar with yolks and add vanilla. Scald milk and cream. While stirring, gradually add the milk mixture to the egg mixture. Pour into small baking cups. Place in pan with water halfway up the sides of the cups. Bake 30 minutes at 350 degrees until firm. Cool. Before serving, sprinkle brown sugar over the top and place under the broiler to caramelize.

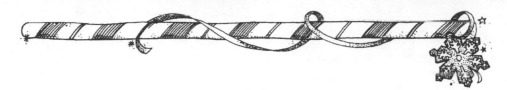

Boston Cream Cake

Have fun experimenting with different pudding flavors...
chocolate, coconut or pistachio.

1 pkg. of 2-layer yellow cake mix, plus required ingredients listed on box	1 large pkg. instant vanilla pudding 16-oz. container chocolate frosting

Make the cake according to directions in 2 round layers. Cool and remove from pans. Make the pudding while cake is baking and refrigerate. When cake is cooled, place a layer on a pretty dish. Spread the pudding over this, but stay about one inch away from the edges. This will keep it from running over the edge when you put the second layer on. Place second layer on top. Open frosting container and peel off the foil. Place lid back on and microwave at 20 second intervals, stirring between, until frosting is pourable but not boiling (the consistency of thick syrup). Let cool a few moments and then spoon over the top of the cake until the top is covered and it runs down the sides.

To decorate:

Put a maraschino cherry in the center. If desired, put green spearmint leaves and cherries cut in half around the top edge of the cake or the edge of the plate. Refrigerate until serving time.

For an inexpensive, but much-appreciated gift for a busy mom, offer to do some of her Christmas shopping. Agree ahead of time on what items you are to shop for, what price range, and work out the payment for the items. This could be a life-saver for a mom who can't find time without the kids to shop for Christmas surprises. Just about anyone would appreciate having someone else fight the crowds for them.

Peanut Butter Chocolate Chip Cheesecake

A rich and creamy cheesecake-lover's dream.

1-1/4 c. graham cracker crumbs
1/3 c. sugar
1/4 c. cocoa
1/3 c. butter or margarine, melted
3 8-oz. pkgs. cream cheese, softened
1 can sweetened condensed milk

1-2/3 c. peanut butter
  chips, melted
4 eggs, beaten
2 t. vanilla extract
1 c. mini chocolate chips
  (semi-sweet)

Stir together graham cracker crumbs, sugar, cocoa, and butter or margarine and press into the bottom of a 9-inch springform pan. In a large mixer bowl, beat together cream cheese and condensed milk. Add peanut butter chips, eggs, and vanilla extract. Beat well. Add the chocolate chips and pour over crust. Bake 55 to 60 minutes at 325 degrees until center is set. (Hint: Usually the top splits when the cheesecake is done. Tap the sides very gently...if it shakes, keep on baking.) Cool and refrigerate. Garnish as desired.

Spicy Doughnut Puffs

The warm, wonderful aroma will fill your kitchen!

2 c. biscuit mix
1/4 c. sugar
1/2 t. cinnamon
1/2 t. nutmeg

2 large eggs, slightly beaten
1/3 c. milk
1 t. vanilla

Combine biscuit mix, sugar and spices in a bowl. Add eggs, milk, and vanilla. Stir well. Heat at least one inch of cooking oil in a frying pan or use a deep fryer according to instructions; heat oil to 400 degrees. Drop small mounds of dough into the hot oil until golden brown. Drain on paper towels. While still hot, shake in a bag with 3/4 cup sugar and one teaspoon of cinnamon. Remove from the bag and enjoy while still warm, or cool and store in an airtight container. Makes 36.

Christmas Eve Cream Puffs
Rich and dreamy!

1/2 c. butter
1 c. water
1/4 t. salt
1 c. white flour

4 large eggs
16-oz. container of chocolate
    fudge frosting for topping

In a 2-quart saucepan, heat the butter, water, and salt until the butter melts. Remove from heat and immediately stir in the flour with a wooden spoon. When a ball forms, beat in one egg. Do this until all the eggs are beaten in and you have a large, satiny ball of dough. (This is time-consuming, but be patient. If you do this one at a time, the eggs will go in.) Preheat the oven to 400 degrees. Makes 15 to 20 puffs, depending on the size you want. Grease a large cookie sheet or two smaller ones. You can use an ice cream scoop to get them uniformly sized. Put small amounts on the pans and bake them for 30 to 35 minutes or until risen and golden brown. Slide off carefully and stick each one with a toothpick in one or two places. This lets out the steam and keeps the puffs up. Let cool while you make the filling.

Ricotta filling:

1 lb. ricotta cheese
1/3 c. sugar
1/4 c. mini chocolate chips
1 t. orange zest

2 T. coffee liqueur
(alternate: use 1/4 c.
    strong coffee;
    almost as good)

Mix all ingredients with a beater until smooth. When puffs are cool, cut off the top three quarters of the way, making a little flap, so you can flip it back enough to fill it. Put a spoonful of filling in each one. Put the top back in place. Then make or buy your favorite chocolate frosting. Microwave it 15 seconds and stir it until it is almost runny. Spoon a bit over top of each puff (like an eclair). You can put a candied cherry on top, or just before serving, sprinkle with powdered sugar. (Snow on the roof!)

Hot Pudding Cake

Served warm on a cold winter evening, this really satisfies!

Cake:

1 c. flour	1/2 c. milk
2/3 c. sugar	1/4 c. butter, melted
1/4 c. unsweetened cocoa	1-1/2 t. vanilla
2 t. baking powder	

Topping:

2/3 c. sugar	1-1/4 c. strong hot coffee
1/4 c. unsweetened cocoa	whipped cream

Preheat oven to 350 degrees. Butter an 8-inch square baking dish. In a mixing bowl, whisk together flour, sugar, cocoa and baking powder. Whisk in milk, melted butter and vanilla until well blended. Batter will be quite stiff. Spread in prepared baking dish. To make topping, combine sugar and cocoa, then sprinkle evenly over cake batter. Pour hot coffee over top of batter. Do not stir. Bake 35 to 40 minutes, until top is glazed and dark brown and cake is bubbling up in places. Cool on a rack for at least one hour. Serve warm or at room temperature with whipped cream. Makes 6 to 8 servings.

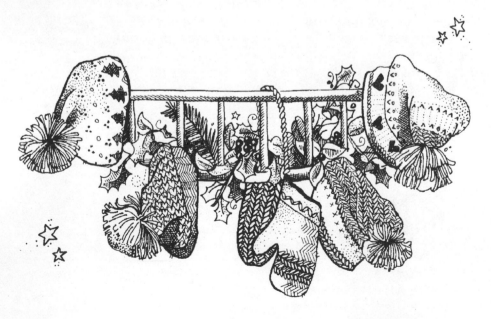

Pumpkin Spice Cake

Yummy with whipped cream or vanilla ice cream on top.

1-1/2 c. flour
1/4 c. sugar
1/2 c. butter
32-oz. can pumpkin
3 eggs, beaten
14-oz. can evaporated milk
1/2 t. cinnamon

1/4 t. cloves
1/2 t. salt
1 c. sugar
scant 1/2 c. butter
1 box single layer yellow
　cake mix
1/2 c. nuts, chopped (optional)

Combine flour and sugar, and cut butter into it until butter is the size of peas. Press into a 13"x9" pan. Combine pumpkin, eggs, evaporated milk, cinnamon, cloves, salt, and sugar. Pour over unbaked crust. Cut butter into cake mix and add nuts. Sprinkle over unbaked filling. Bake at 350 degrees for 60 to 65 minutes. Cool, then chill in refrigerator (unless you want to serve warm with ice cream).

Mousse de Café

A quick, creamy, cool dessert.

1 c. whipped topping
1/2 t. instant coffee powder
1/4 c. coffee liqueur
2 T. sugar

1 egg white
2 t. sugar
chocolate sprinkles

Chill bowl and beaters. Combine whipped topping and coffee powder. Beat until stiff. Add coffee liqueur and 2 tablespoons sugar. Beat until very stiff. Beat egg white to soft peaks. Add 2 teaspoons sugar and beat until stiff. Fold egg white into cream mixture. Chill.

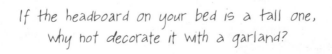

If the headboard on your bed is a tall one, why not decorate it with a garland?

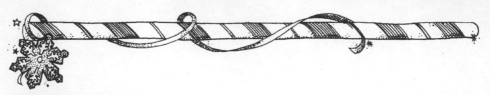

Christmas Fruit Tarts

In just 15 minutes, you can whip up this elegant dessert for 30 people!

21-oz. can fruit pie filling (try cranberry or cherry)

2 pkgs. phyllo dough shells
1 container whipped topping

Thaw phyllo dough shells according to package directions. Fill each shell with about one tablespoon of pie filling. Bake filled shells 5 to 8 minutes at 375 degrees. Cool slightly. Top each dessert cup with a generous dollop of whipped topping. Serve immediately. Makes 30 dessert cups.

Make snow days extra special for the kids...
tell stories, go sledding, make cocoa, sing Christmas carols,
watch Christmas movies and wrap presents.

Aunt Libby's Pumpkin-Rum Pie

You may need to make several of these pies...they don't last!

9" unbaked pie crust
3 eggs
1/2 c. brown sugar
1/2 t. salt
1-1/2 c. heavy cream

1 c. canned pumpkin
1/4 c. rum
1 t. cinnamon
1/2 t. ground cloves
1/4 t. mace

Topping:
1 c. whipped cream

1 T. rum

Preheat oven to 400 degrees. Mix all filling ingredients together and pour into pie shell. Bake for 35 minutes. Test the filling by sticking a silver knife in the center...if it comes out clean, the pie is ready. When entirely cooled, pipe sweetened whipped cream, flavored with rum, all over the top.

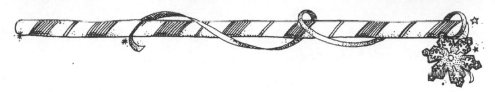

Hot Cocoa Cake

The warmth and coziness of hot chocolate on a plate!

1/2 c. shortening
3/4 c. sugar
2 eggs
1-1/2 c. unbleached
   white flour

3/4 t. salt
2 t. baking powder
2/3 c. milk
8 T. or 2 packets of instant
   hot cocoa

Cream together shortening, sugar, and eggs until mixture is fluffy. Add flour, salt, and baking powder alternately with milk, beating well after each addition. Spoon 1/3 of batter into a well-greased 6-1/2 cup bundt pan. Sprinkle one of the packets of hot cocoa mix evenly over the batter. Add the second 1/3 of batter and sprinkle with remaining hot cocoa mix. Top with the rest of the batter and spread evenly in pan. Bake at 350 degrees for 35 minutes or until a toothpick comes out clean. Let stand 5 minutes and turn out onto serving plate. Delicious served warm as a coffee cake, or let cool and dust with a little powdered sugar. If desired, add chopped nuts of any kind in the layers with the hot cocoa mix.

Aunt Mary's Coconut Coffee Twist

If you have house guests, they'll love this with their morning coffee.

1 pkg. dry yeast
4 T. sugar
1/4 c. warm water
3-1/2 c. flour
1 t. salt
1/2 c. butter

3 egg yolks, beaten
1 c. light cream
1/2 c. powdered sugar
1-1/2 T. milk
1/2 c. flaked coconut

Stir yeast and 2 teaspoons sugar into water. Combine flour, salt, and remaining sugar in a bowl. Cut butter into flour with pastry blender. Blend egg yolks and cream, then stir into flour mixture. Add yeast mixture; blend, cover and chill for several hours. On a floured surface, divide dough into 6 equal pieces. Roll each into a 12-inch long rope. Twist 2 ropes together, pinching ends to make a ring. Repeat to make 3 rings. Place each in a greased pie plate, and let rise 2 hours or until nearly doubled. Bake in a 350 degree oven for 30 minutes. Make an icing by blending powdered sugar and milk. Sprinkle with coconut. Serve warm with your favorite coffee, tea, or hot chocolate.

Most of us have at least one treasured antique silver serving spoon. Why not display it?
Add a tiny bit of greenery and some ribbon to the bottom of the handle, near the bowl, and set it out for all to see and admire. The handles are usually so pretty, and the decorations dress them up even more for the holidays.

Christmas Dessert Surprise

This looks like a plain dessert, but hidden inside is a chocolate, minty surprise.

1 pkg. chocolate wafer cookies   **large tub of whipped topping**
hard peppermint candies

Divide the whipped topping equally into two bowls. Crush the peppermints and stir them into one of the bowls of topping. Spread a thin layer of plain whipped topping in a rectangular shape on a platter. Spread a cookie with a layer of the peppermint topping and stand it upright in the whipped topping. Stack each cookie on its side, one closely behind the other. Press the cookies together gently to form a log shape. Spread the log with the plain whipped topping. Put it in the refrigerator for several hours before serving so the wafers become soft. This can be sliced diagonally from one corner to the other to show the layers.

Mom's Christmas Morning Cranberry Puffs

Or, make as a Christmas Eve treat and leave one for Santa.

3/4 c. cranberries, chopped   **1/4 c. sugar**
1/2 c. sugar   **1 egg**
1 c. biscuit mix   **1/3 c. milk**

Heat oven to 400 degrees. Toss cranberries lightly with 1/2 cup sugar and divide among 8 large muffin cups, greased. Mix remaining ingredients. Beat vigorously 1/2 minute. Fill muffin cups 2/3 full. Bake about 15 minutes until golden brown. Invert muffins onto wire racks. Serve warm topped with hot butter sauce. Makes 8 servings.

Butter Sauce:

1/2 c. sugar   **1/4 c. butter, softened**
1/4 c. light cream   **1/2 t. vanilla**

Heat 1/2 cup sugar and light cream to boiling, stirring constantly. Remove from heat; beat in butter, softened with rotary beater. Stir in vanilla. Pour over cranberry puffs and serve in dessert dishes.

Merry Berry Almond Glazed Sour Cream Cake

Red berries peeking through the almonds make this a particularly festive-looking cake.

2 c. flour
1 t. baking powder
1 t. baking soda
1/2 t. salt
1/2 c. butter or
   margarine, softened
1 c. sugar

2 eggs
2 t. almond extract
1-1/2 c. sour cream
16-oz. can whole
   cranberry sauce
1/2 c. almonds, chopped

Glaze:

3/4 c. powdered sugar
1/2 t. almond extract

2 T. warm water

Preheat oven to 350 degrees. Grease and flour a 10-inch tube pan. Mix flour, baking powder, soda, and salt together and set aside. Cream butter and sugar together, beating well. Add eggs one at a time, beating very well after each is added. Mix in almond extract. Stir in flour mixture, alternating with the sour cream. Spoon half of the batter into the prepared tube pan. Spoon half of the cranberry sauce over the batter and swirl slightly. Spoon remaining batter over swirled cranberry sauce. Cover this batter with remaining cranberry sauce, swirling slightly. Sprinkle with almonds. Bake at 350 degrees for 45 to 55 minutes, until firm. Cool 10 minutes and carefully remove from pan and glaze.

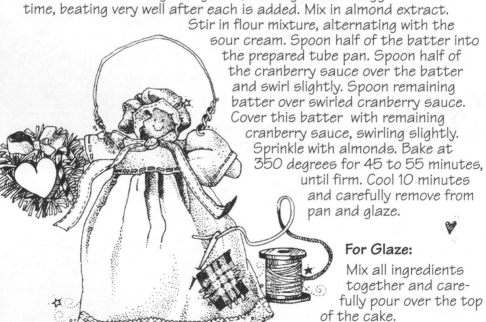

For Glaze:

Mix all ingredients together and carefully pour over the top of the cake.

Granny's Apple-Cranberry Tart

The perfect pie for Christmas dinner.

Pastry:

2/3 c. walnuts, chopped	1/4 t. salt
1 c. flour	1/3 c. cold butter,
2 T. sugar	sliced into pieces
1/4 t. cinnamon	2 or 3 T. ice water

Filling:

2 T. flour	1 c. fresh cranberries
1/3 c. plus 2 T. sugar	2 t. orange zest grated
3 Granny Smith apples,	1/4 c. orange juice
peeled and thinly sliced	1 t. cornstarch

To make the crust, process walnuts in a food processor until coarsely ground. Add flour, sugar, cinnamon and salt and process until just mixed. Add butter and pulse until mixture resembles small course crumbs. With food processor running, add the ice water to form dough. Remove dough, form into a ball and flatten into a circle. Wrap in plastic and refrigerate for 30 minutes. While crust is chilling, preheat oven to 375 degrees and prepare filling. In mixing bowl, combine flour, and 2 tablespoons. sugar. Toss with apples and set aside. Roll out dough and pat into a 9-inch tart pan. Spoon in apple mixture and bake for 25 minutes. While baking, combine cranberries, orange zest, orange juice, cornstarch and remaining sugar. Cook cranberry mixture at medium-low heat until it boils and thickens. Remove from heat and spoon over baked apple tart. Bake for another 10 minutes until apples are tender. Allow to cool. Serve with a dollop of whipped cream and sprinkle of cinnamon.

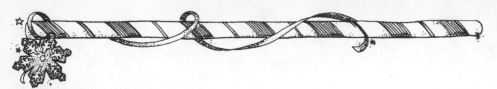

Pumpkin Dutch Apple Pie

Two favorite flavors in one wonderful pie.

Apple Layer:

2 medium Granny Smith
   apples, peeled, cored,
   and thinly sliced
1/4 c. sugar
2 t. all-purpose flour

1 t. lemon juice
1/4 t. cinnamon
9" deep-dish pie shell,
   unbaked

Toss apples with sugar, flour, lemon juice, and cinnamon. Place in a pie shell.

Pumpkin Layer:

2 eggs, lightly beaten
1-1/2 c. solid-pack pumpkin
1 c. undiluted evaporated milk
1/2 c. sugar

2 T. butter, melted
3/4 t. ground cinnamon
1/8 t. ground nutmeg
1/4 t. salt

Crumble Topping:

1/2 c. all-purpose flour
5 T. sugar

3 T. butter, softened
1/3 c. walnuts, chopped

Combine eggs, pumpkin, evaporated milk, sugar, butter, cinnamon, nutmeg and salt. Pour over apples. Bake in preheated oven at 375 degrees for 30 minutes. While pie is baking, mix together ingredients for crumble topping. Remove pie from oven and sprinkle with topping. Return to oven and bake for an additional 20 minutes or until custard is set. Cool.

Crunchy apples

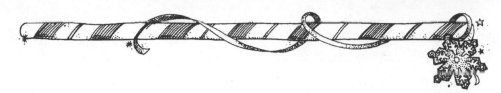

Apple-Pecan Upside-Down Pie

We love this version of a classic, especially with a scoop of ice cream!.

1/3 c. sugar
2 T. flour
1/2 t. cinnamon
1/4 c. butter, softened

1/2 c. pecan halves
1/2 c. brown sugar, packed
2 9" pie crusts
5 c. apples, peeled and sliced

In a small bowl, combine sugar, flour and cinnamon. Set aside. In the bottom of a pie plate; spread the butter evenly around the bottom and sides. Push pecans (rounded side down) into the butter. Pat brown sugar evenly over pecans. Place one pie crust over the brown sugar and press gently. Trim off any excess crust around edge. Arrange half of the apples and follow again with sugar. Cut small openings in the remaining crust to vent. Place crust on top, trim edge and pinch edges together. Cover edges of crust with foil to prevent over-browning. Bake for 20 minutes, then remove foil. Bake for another 20 minutes, until the apples are tender. Cool for 5 to 10 minutes, and then invert onto a serving plate. Wonderful when served warm.

For a special mother-daughter memory, take an evening for yourselves right before Christmas. Have a leisurely dinner at a favorite restaurant, exchange little gifts or goodies, then attend a holiday concert. The break from all the hustle and bustle of Christmas will refresh both of you, and spending that very special evening together will become an important part of Christmas every year.

Seven Layer Bars

This recipe is easily doubled for a 13"x9" pan.

1 stick margarine or butter
1 c. graham cracker crumbs
6 oz. chocolate chips
1 c. coconut, flaked
6 oz. butterscotch chips

1 can condensed
   sweetened milk
1 c. walnuts or pecans,
   chopped

In a small glass pan (approximately 11"x7"), put melted margarine or butter. Sprinkle graham cracker crumbs to coat the bottom. Evenly spread out the chocolate chips, then coconut, then butterscotch chips. Pour the condensed milk over top to coat evenly. Top with nuts. Bake at 325 degrees for 25 to 30 minutes. Cool until almost cold and then cut with a knife or pizza cutter into small bars.

If you have small children and curious pets around the house, tie jingle bells onto the lower branches of your tree with some red ribbon. When you hear the sound of bells, you'll know that either the cat or the children are close to the tree and it's time to come running! Also, just in case the little ones try to pull the tree over, you can tie it to a hook in the ceiling or wall with some strong fishing line.

White Hot Chocolate

Serve in thick mugs with whipped cream, a dash of cinnamon or cocoa powder and a candy cane.

3 c. half and half
2/3 c. vanilla chips
3" cinnamon stick
1/8 t. ground nutmeg

1 t. vanilla
1/4 t. almond extract
ground cinnamon

In a saucepan, combine 1/4 cup of the half and half, vanilla chips, stick cinnamon and nutmeg. Whisk over low heat until vanilla chips are melted. Remove stick cinnamon. Add remaining half and half. Whisk until heated throughout. Remove from heat and add vanilla and almond extract.

Makes 4 or 5 servings.

Mom's Coconut Bars

It's a very special mom who creates these cookies!

2 c. graham cracker crumbs
1/4 c. powdered sugar
1/2 c. melted butter
2-1/3 c. flaked coconut

1 can sweetened
    condensed milk
12-oz. pkg. chocolate chips
6 T. butter

Combine graham cracker crumbs, sugar and butter and press into an ungreased 13"x9" pan; bake for 10 minutes at 325 degrees. Combine coconut and condensed milk and spread over baked layer. Return and bake for 10 to 12 minutes at 325 degrees. While the two layers are cooling slightly, melt the chocolate chips and the butter over low heat, stirring to blend. Then spread over the coconut layer and cool. Cut into bars. Refrigerate or freeze until served.

Homemade Pretzels
Just like they sell on New York City street corners.

2 pkgs. dry yeast	1 t. salt
1-1/2 c. warm water, not hot	1 egg, beaten
2 T. sugar	Kosher salt
4 c. white flour, approximately	

Mix yeast, water, and sugar in a bowl. Let sit approximately 20 minutes until frothy. If it doesn't get frothy, your water was too hot and you killed the yeast. Try again. Add flour and salt. Flour your hands and work the dough until you have a soft, smooth, (no longer sticky) dough. Break off a piece and roll it between your palms until you have a 6-inch rope. Shape into a pretzel form on a lightly greased cookie sheet. Beat the egg with one tablespoon water and brush each pretzel. Then sprinkle with coarse salt or Kosher salt. Bake at 425 degrees for 12 to 15 minutes until golden brown. Eat warm, or reheat later in the microwave.

Out-of-This-World Fudge Topping
A real treat for the chocolate-lover, but don't count the calories.

1/2 c. butter	7 oz. marshmallow cream
3/4 c. cocoa	1 t. vanilla extract
2 c. sugar	1 c. walnuts, chopped
1/8 t. salt	vegetable spray
3/4 c. evaporated milk	

In a 4-quart saucepan sprayed with vegetable spray, melt butter over low heat. Stir in the cocoa and add sugar, salt, and evaporated milk. Stir until well-blended. Add marshmallow cream and bring to a boil. Continue stirring and boiling for about 5 minutes. Remove from the heat and stir in the vanilla. Cool about 20 minutes and beat with a wooden spoon. Stir in the walnuts. Spoon into small jars and refrigerate. When ready to serve, set jar in a little hot water until it is pourable. Serve over ice cream or angel food cake.

Nana's Sour Cream Cut-Out Cookies

A yummy, rich addition to your Christmas cookie tray.

1 c. white sugar
1 c. real butter
2 eggs
1 c. dairy sour cream
   (do not use light or
   fat-free in this recipe)

1 t. baking soda
pinch of salt
4-1/2 or 5 c. flour
1 T. vanilla extract
1/4 t. ground nutmeg

Cream sugar and butter together. Add eggs, sour cream, and remaining ingredients. Chill dough at least eight hours. Roll 1/4 to 1/2-inch thick and cut with desired shaped cutters. Bake at 350 degrees 8 to 10 minutes. Do not let these brown too much on the bottoms. Cool and frost if desired.

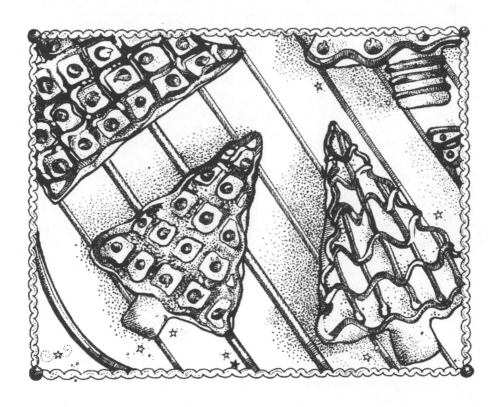

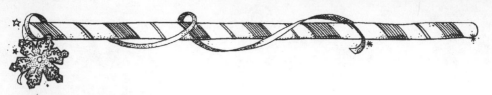

Christmas Holly Leaves

Even the smallest elf can add the red cinnamon candies to the leaves.

1 pkg. large marshmallows
   (about 60)
1 c. butter
1 t. vanilla extract

3 t. green food coloring
7 c. corn flakes
red cinnamon candies,
   1 or 2 per leaf clump

In a heavy 4-quart saucepan, melt marshmallows and butter over low heat, stirring constantly. Add vanilla and food coloring and stir until well-blended. Fold in corn flakes. Drop by rounded buttered table-spoons onto wax paper-lined cookie sheets. Shape into 2-inch wreaths, or just little "clumps" of leaves. Decorate each with candies. Do not freeze. Makes about 50. This little "candy cookie" is tasty and looks great on your holiday cookie platter. It's similar to rice cereal bars, but the corn flakes give it another texture.

Russian Tea Cakes

Make these bite-sized, so there's no powdered sugar falling on a fancy dress or tie!

1 c. butter, softened
1/2 c. powdered sugar, sifted
1 t. vanilla
2-1/4 c. all-purpose flour, sifted
1/4 t. salt

3/4 c. nuts, finely chopped
   (pecans are a nice change
   from walnuts)
powdered sugar for coating

Mix together butter, powdered sugar, and vanilla. Combine flour and salt, then stir into butter mixture. Mix in nuts. Chill dough. Roll into one-inch balls. Place on ungreased cookie sheets (cookies do not spread, but they do "puff up" and seem a bit larger). Bake at 400 degrees until set, but not brown. While still warm, roll in powdered sugar. Cool, then roll in sugar again. Store in an air-tight container with a little leftover powdered sugar. When put on a serving plate, just gently turn the container upside down a few times to recoat. They'll stay all fluffy and white.

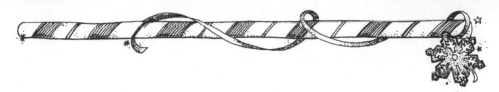

Pumpkin Madeleines

A fun way to enjoy the warm flavors of pumpkin and spice!

2 eggs
2/3 c. sugar
1/2 c. butter, melted
1 T. flour

1 c. flour
2 T. canned pumpkin
1 t. lemon juice
1/4 t. pumpkin pie spice

Preheat oven to 375 degrees. In a small bowl, beat eggs and sugar at high speed until light and fluffy, approximately 5 minutes. Meanwhile, pour 2 tablespoons of melted butter into another small bowl. Blend in one tablespoon flour. Brush molds with this butter-flour mixture to prevent cookies from sticking. Beat one cup flour into egg mixture at low speed. Slowly beat in remaining butter. Beat in pumpkin, lemon juice and pumpkin pie spice at medium speed until well-blended. Fill prepared molds with batter, using about 1-1/2 tablespoons for each. Do not spread batter out in molds. Bake for 15 to 20 minutes or until golden brown. Remove from pans at once and cool on rack. Madeleines are best eaten within a few hours of baking. Or, wrap and freeze for up to 8 weeks.

Yield: 20 madeleines.

Frog Leg Candy

This candy is very easy and takes very little time; it's a fun recipe for kids.

3 c. semi-sweet chocolate chips
12-oz. pkg. butterscotch chips

1 large bag chow mein noodles
1-1/2 c. walnut pieces

Using low power, melt the chips in a bowl in the microwave, stirring halfway through. Add the chow mein noodles (smash the bag slightly so they're not too large) and the walnuts. Stir to cover the crunchy items with the melted mixture. Drop tablespoonfuls onto wax paper and allow to harden. Store in a covered container.

Aunt Margaret's Apricot Fold-ups

An overnight success!

8-oz. pkg. dried apricots
8-oz. pkg. cream cheese,
   softened

1 c. butter, softened
2 c. all-purpose flour
1 c. sugar

Soak apricots overnight in cold water. Mix cream cheese, butter, and flour thoroughly, like pie crust. Divide into 3 balls and chill overnight. Cook apricots slowly until soft and thick with just enough water to cover. Stir in sugar. Put aside to cool before using. Roll dough out thin on floured board. Cut into about 3-1/2 inch squares. Spoon in a teaspoon of apricot mixture, fold and seal. (Fold by bringing up edges and making a little square. Pinch together, sealing tightly.) Bake in 425 degree oven on an ungreased cookie sheet until golden brown. Glaze with a powdered sugar icing; just drizzle over fold-ups while warm.

Easy powdered sugar icing:

A little butter, a little milk, a lot of powdered sugar. Not too stiff, just loose enough to drizzle.

Deep Dish Brownies

They almost taste like fudge!

1 c. and 2 T. butter, melted
2-1/4 c. sugar
2 t. vanilla
4 eggs
1-1/8 c. flour

3/4 c. cocoa
3/4 t. baking powder
3/4 t. salt
1-3/4 c. semi-sweet
   chocolate chips

Heat oven to 350 degrees. Grease a 13"x9" pan. In a medium mixing bowl, blend butter, sugar, and vanilla. Add eggs and beat well with a spoon. In a separate bowl, combine flour, cocoa, baking powder, and salt. Gradually add to egg mixture. Beat well until blended. Stir in chocolate chips and spread in prepared pan. Bake 40 to 45 minutes or until brownies begin to pull away from sides of pan. Cool completely and cut into squares.

Holiday Quickie Cookie

When the kids just can't wait!

3 c. biscuit mix
1 c. sugar
1 large egg
1/3 c. water

1 t. vanilla or almond extract
1/4 c. maraschino cherries,
    chopped and drained
1/4 c. chocolate chips

Mix biscuit mix and sugar. Add egg, water, and flavoring. Mix well. Stir in cherries and chips. This is especially pretty if you use red and green cherries. Drop from tablespoons onto an ungreased cookie sheet. Bake at 375 degrees for 10 to 12 minutes. Cool on racks.

Yield: About 4 dozen cookies.

Sugar Cookies

These are very easy-the kind even a small child can help make.

1 c. butter
2 c. sugar
2 eggs

2 t. vanilla
4 t. baking powder
3-1/2 c. flour

Cream together butter and sugar. Add eggs and vanilla. Sift together baking powder and flour and add to creamed mixture. Roll to 1/8-inch thick on floured board. Cut with a floured cutter. Sprinkle with sugar or frost later. Bake at 350 degrees for 8 to 10 minutes on an ungreased cookie sheet.

Yield: 3 to 4 dozen cookies.

Caramel Cookie Cups

Very rich...an elegant treat with coffee or tea.

Cups:

8-oz. pkg. cream cheese, softened

2 sticks margarine, softened
2 c. flour

Mix cream cheese and margarine by hand. Add flour and mix until smooth. Form dough into 42 to 45 walnut-sized balls. Press dough balls into mini muffin pans, making sure dough is pressed up the sides. Bake 15 to 20 minutes at 350 degrees. Remove from pan to cookie sheet.

Filling:

14-oz. bag caramels
1/2 c. evaporated milk

Melt caramels and evaporated milk in top of double boiler or in microwave. When melted, fill cups and cool.

Icing:

1/2 c. shortening
1/2 c. margarine
2/3 c. granulated sugar
3/4 c. evaporated milk
1 t. vanilla
1 c. walnuts, finely chopped

In medium-sized bowl, beat shortening, margarine and sugar until light. Add evaporated milk and vanilla; beat until fluffy and sugar is dissolved. Ice cookies and sprinkle with chopped walnuts.

Note: The cookie looks much more elegant if the icing is piped on with a decorator's tube.

Christmas Ho Ho's

A fun treat for a holiday party.

1 c. chocolate chips
1/4 c. shortening
2 c. walnuts, chopped

50 small candy canes
10-oz. pkg. large marshmallows

Place chocolate chips and shortening in a 2-cup measure. Micro-wave at 50% power for 1-1/2 to 3 minutes or until chips are shiny and soft. Stir until smooth. Place chopped nuts in a shallow dish. Insert a small candy cane into each marshmallow center and dip the end of marshmallow into melted chocolate. Immediately dip into nuts and set on its side on wax paper. Repeat. Continue this process until all 50 Ho Ho's are done. If your children don't like chopped nuts, you can dip them in rainbow sprinkles. Store in covered container.

Apricot-Nut Supreme Brownies

Really different, rich and tasty!

4 oz. chocolate chips or baking
    chocolate (white or dark)
1/3 c. butter
1/2 c. sugar
2 eggs
1/4 t. almond extract

3/4 c. flour
1/2 t. baking powder
1/4 t. salt
1 c. dried apricots, quartered
1/2 c. almonds, slivered

In a large saucepan, melt chocolate and butter over low heat. Add sugar, eggs, and extract. Stir quickly to blend. In a separate bowl, stir flour, baking powder and salt. Stir into chocolate mixture. Add 1/2 cup apricots and 1/4 cup slivered almonds. Stir to blend. Pour into greased 11"x7" pan. Sprinkle with remaining apricot quarters and almonds. Bake for 25 minutes in 350 degree oven or until brownies begin to pull away from the edge of the pan. For optional garnish, drizzle melted white or dark chocolate over brownies. Or place a brownie in a brandy snifter, cover with a scoop of vanilla ice cream and top with a splash of apricot liqueur.

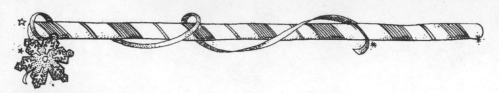

Spirited Raisin Cookies

Give your cookies some holiday spirit with rum-flavored raisins.

1/2 c. raisins
1/2 c. warm rum
   (or 3 T. rum extract
   in 1/2 c. warm water)
1 c. butter, softened

1/2 c. powdered sugar, sifted
2 c. flour
1/4 t. salt
1/4 t. baking powder

Bring raisins to boil in rum. Remove from heat. Cover and let stand 30 minutes. Drain. Cream butter and sugar. Sift flour with salt and baking powder. Add gradually to creamed mixture. Add raisins. Roll out dough to 1/2-inch thickness on floured board. Cut with cookie cutters. Decorate with cookie stamps (optional). Bake at 375 degrees 20 minutes.

Makes 12 cookies.

cookie Cutters

Most of us, young or old, "can't wait" until Christmas! However, Christmas is not just a day, but a season. Let's make the most of it by spreading out the parties and special treats over an extended period. The season can be extended by celebrating old-fashioned days such as Boxing Day or Saint Lucia's Day... this can help us learn more about the history and spirit of the season, while creating some pretty great memories.

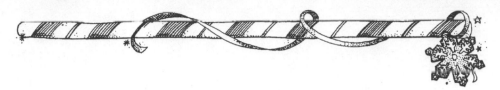

Aunt Libby's Eggnog Cookies

Another way to enjoy your holiday eggnog!

1/4 c. unsalted butter
6 T. sugar
1 egg yolk
1 T. dark rum
1 T. whipping cream

3/4 c. cake flour
1/4 t. baking powder
dash salt
1/4 t. ground cinnamon

Cream butter and sugar in medium-sized bowl until light. Beat in egg yolk, rum, and whipping cream. Stir together cake flour, baking powder, salt and cinnamon in a separate bowl. Stir into egg yolk mixture. Drop batter by heaping tablespoons onto ungreased baking sheet 2 inches apart. Bake at 350 degrees until cookies are puffed and lightly browned, 17 to 19 minutes. Allow cookies to set on baking sheet 5 to 10 minutes, then gently remove to wire rack to cool completely.

Makes 10 cookies.

Cranberry Cookies

So tart, tender and crunchy.

3 c. cranberries
3 c. flour
1/4 t. baking soda
1 t. baking powder
1/2 t. salt
1/2 c. butter

1 c. sugar
1 c. brown sugar, packed
1 egg
1/4 c. milk
2 T. lemon juice
1 c. walnuts, chopped

Steam the cranberries 5 minutes and chop coarsely. Sift flour, baking soda, baking powder, and salt together. Cream butter and sugars until light and fluffy, then beat in egg, milk, and lemon juice. Stir in the flour mixture bit by bit. Add the cranberries and nuts. The cranberries will be soft and create a marbleized pattern in the dough. Drop by teaspoonfuls onto greased cookie sheets, one inch apart. Bake at 375 degrees for about 15 minutes, until firm and golden. Remove to racks to cool.

Makes about 90 cookies.

Grandma Mac's Plum Cookies

Sweet plums give these cookies extra moisture and texture.

3/4 c. unsalted butter,
   softened
3/4 c. light brown sugar
3 eggs, beaten
4 c. flour, sifted

2 t. baking soda
1/2 t. mace
1/2 t. allspice
2 c. ripe sweet plums,
   peeled and coarsely chopped

Preheat the oven to 350 degrees. Lightly grease 2 large baking sheets with butter or vegetable shortening. In a large mixing bowl, cream together butter and sugar. Beat in the eggs and mix well. Sift the flour with the baking soda, mace, and allspice. Add the flour mixture to the batter one cup at a time. Stir in the plums. Drop rounded teaspoonfuls of batter onto the baking sheets, about 2 inches apart. Bake for about 15 minutes or until the cookies have browned around the edges.

Very Simple Chocolate Chip Tart Cups

So much fun to fill! Perfect for ice cream...
you get to eat the cup.

2 T. butter or margarine,
   softened

16-oz. tube chocolate
   chip cookie dough

Grease small or medium-sized muffin tin cups, depending on the size of tart you wish to make. Remove cookie dough from refrigerator. While still cold, slice into 1/4 to 1/2-inch thick slices. Butter hands and roll each slice to form a ball. When dough gets a little soft, press evenly into bottom and up sides of muffin tin cups. Follow directions on tube of cookie dough for baking...keep an eye on them. As they bake, the bottoms will puff up a bit, but there is plenty of room for a filling. Fill with vanilla pudding topped with whipped cream, or a scoop of ice cream with chocolate sauce and nuts.

Makes approximately 20 tarts.

Red Raspberry Oatmeal Gems

Experiment with other jam flavors such as strawberry, blackberry and peach. Yum!

1 c. margarine
1/2 c. brown sugar, packed
1/2 c. white sugar
2 eggs
1 t. vanilla

1-1/2 c. flour
1 t. soda
1/2 t. cinnamon
3 c. rolled oats
red raspberry jam

Cream margarine and sugars until light and fluffy. Blend in eggs and vanilla. Combine flour, soda, and cinnamon; add to creamed mixture. Mix well. Stir in oats. Drop heaping teaspoonfuls of dough onto ungreased cookie sheets. Indent centers. Fill with 1/4 teaspoon jam. Bake at 375 degrees for 8 to 10 minutes or until golden brown.

Fancy Flower Biscuits

Kids love to help make these for breakfast.

1 can of 10 refrigerator biscuits
3 T. butter or margarine,
   melted
1/3 c. sugar

1/2 t. cinnamon
1/4 t. nutmeg
maraschino cherry halves,
   well-drained

Cut through each biscuit from outside edge 3/4 of the way to the center in 5 places. This forms 5 petals for flower. Mix sugar, cinnamon, and nutmeg together. Dip each biscuit flower into melted butter, then sugar mixture. Place on ungreased cookie sheet. Garnish each flower biscuit in center with a maraschino cherry half. Bake at 350 degrees for 12 to 14 minutes until golden brown. Serve flowers warm.

15-Minute Macaroons

So quick and easy...coco-nutty!

1-1/3 c. flaked coconut   **1/3 c. sweetened condensed milk**
1/2 t. vanilla

Combine all ingredients, mixing well. Drop from teaspoonfuls one inch apart onto well-greased baking sheet. Bake at 350 degrees for 10 to 12 minutes or until golden brown. Remove at once from baking sheet. To make chocolate macaroons, fold in one-inch square melted semi-sweet chocolate before baking.

Makes approximately two dozen.

Easy Cream Cheese Truffles

It's fun rolling these in the different coatings.

8-oz. pkg. cream cheese,   **1/4 c. almonds, toasted and**
  softened   **finely chopped**
4 c. powdered sugar   **1/4 c. sweetened cocoa powder**
5 oz. unsweetened chocolate,   **1/4 c. powdered sugar**
  melted and cooled   **1/4 c. coconut flakes, toasted**

Beat cream cheese until fluffy. Slowly add powdered sugar. Beat until smooth. Add melted chocolate and beat until blended. Chill for approximately one hour. Shape chilled mixture into one-inch balls. Roll some in powdered sugar, some in cocoa, some in nuts, and some in coconut. Store in an airtight container in the refrigerator for two weeks.

Invite friends over for an address-the-Christmas-cards party.
Ask them to bring a snack to share along with their
cards, stamps, address books and return labels.
Try to have this event as early in the season as possible.
The week after Thanksgiving would be a good time.

Snowballs with Peppermint

A cool winter confection.

1 c. butter
1/2 c. powdered sugar
2 t. peppermint, vanilla, or
    almond extract
2-1/4 c. flour

1/4 t. salt
3/4 c. ground walnuts
    and almonds
peppermint candies
powdered sugar, for coating

Cream butter until light; add sugar. Mix until light and fluffy. Stir in extract. Add dry ingredients. Blend in ground nuts. Shape into walnut-sized balls. Bake on ungreased sheet at 350 degrees for 15 minutes. Immediately after removing from cookie sheet, roll in powdered sugar. Cool and roll in sugar again. Place a nice white paper doily on a pretty pedestal cake plate. Arrange white snowballs on plate. Garnish by scattering peppermint candies and fresh sprigs of pine or holly.

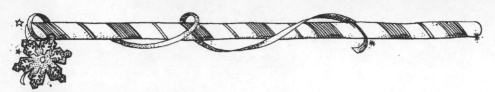

Chocolate Malt Cookies

The flavor of an old-time soda shop.

1 c. butter-flavored shortening
1-1/4 c. brown sugar
1/2 c. malt powder
2 T. chocolate syrup
1 T. vanilla
1 egg

2 c. flour
1 t. soda
1/2 t. salt
1-1/2 c. semi-sweet
   chocolate chunks
1 c. (6 oz.) milk chocolate chips

Combine first five ingredients and beat two minutes. Add egg. Combine flour, soda and salt. Gradually add to malt mixture. Stir in chocolate. Shape into 2-inch balls. Bake at 375 degrees for 12 to 14 minutes or until golden brown.

Frosted Sugar Cookies with Pecans

These are pretty at Christmas in different colors.

1 c. margarine
1 c. oil
1 c. sugar
1 c. powdered sugar
1 t. soda
1 t. cream of tartar

2 eggs
1 t. salt
2 t. vanilla
4 c. flour
16 oz. toasted pecans

Mix all ingredients except pecans and drop by teaspoons onto cookie sheet. Arrange a few pecans in each mound of cookie dough. Bake at 350 degrees for 12 to 15 minutes. Frost and sprinkle each cookie with colored sugar. Makes about 36.

Frosting:

1/4 c. butter, softened
1/8 t. salt
2 c. powdered sugar
3 T. cream or milk
1 t. vanilla

Mix all ingredients and beat with a whisk until well blended & creamy.

Cream Cheese Cupcakes

The surprise filling makes these cakes extra special.

Filling:

8 oz. cream cheese
1/3 c. sugar
1 large egg

1/8 t. salt
1 c. chocolate chips

Soften cream cheese a little in microwave and combine with sugar, egg and salt, beating well. Stir in chips.

Cupcakes:

1-1/2 c. flour
1 c. sugar
1/3 c. cocoa powder
1 t. soda
1/2 t. salt

1/3 c. oil
1 c. water
1 T. vinegar
1 t. vanilla

Combine ingredients in order and blend well. Fill Christmas paper cups 2/3 full. Spoon a tablespoon of cheese filling onto each cupcake. Bake at 350 degrees for about 20 minutes. Frost with your favorite cream cheese or sour cream frosting and sprinkle with chocolate chips or jimmies.

Apple Nut Cake

A treat for breakfast, teatime, anytime.

1 c. oil
2 c. sugar
3 eggs
2 c. flour
1 T. vanilla

1-1/2 t. cinnamon
1 t. soda
3 c. apples, diced
1 c. walnuts, chopped
3/4 c. raisins

Combine first seven ingredients in order, blending well. Stir in apples, nuts and raisins. Bake at 350 degrees in sprayed tube pan for about one hour and 10 minutes.

Butter Tarts

These little tarts look beautiful on a doily-lined platter, garnished with fresh whipped cream.

2 prepared refrigerated
   pie crusts, rolled out
   (or your own pie dough)
1 c. brown sugar
2 eggs
2/3 c. dark sweet corn syrup

dash of salt
6 T. butter, melted
2/3 c. currants
2/3 c. pecans, chopped
1 t. lemon juice
1 t. vanilla

Cut out pastry to fit small muffin cups. Line each cup with pie pastry. Combine all remaining ingredients and pour into pastry cups 3/4 full. Bake at 425 degrees for about 15 to 20 minutes.

Makes 24.

☆

Tie a big red bow on the antenna of your car. This makes it easier to find in those crowded parking lots.

☆

Cherry Cake

For a beautiful finish, mix reserved cherry juice with a little powdered sugar and water and drizzle over the top; garnish with chopped cherries and walnuts.

1/2 lb. butter (no substitutes)
2 c. sugar
2 eggs
3 c. flour
2 t. baking powder
16-oz. can evaporated milk

1/2 c. walnuts, chopped
1 t. vanilla
1/2 t. almond extract
1 small bottle of maraschino
    cherries, drained (reserve juice)

Cream butter and sugar. Add eggs. Add dry ingredients alternately with milk. Fold in flavorings, nuts and cherries. Bake at 350 degrees for 55 minutes in a greased and floured tube pan.

Pineapple Cream Trifle

You may assemble this in a large glass trifle bowl for a beautiful presentation.

2 c. powdered sugar
1 stick butter, melted
1 small can crushed pineapple
1/2 c. pecans, chopped
approximately 48 vanilla wafers

1 pt. cream, whipped, or
    prepared whipped topping
grated coconut
several maraschino cherries
    as garnish

Combine sugar, butter, pineapple and nuts. Arrange 16 vanilla wafers in the bottom of a large glass dish or trifle bowl. Cover with pineapple mixture. Cover with whipped cream. Sprinkle with coconut. Repeat. Top with wafers. Cover and let stand overnight in the refrigerator. Before serving, cover with whipped cream. Sprinkle all over with coconut and garnish with cherries.

Makes 16 servings.

Peanut Butter Bars

The chocolate-peanut butter topping can't be beat.

2 c. quick rolled oats
1/2 c. margarine
1/2 c. brown sugar
1/4 c. light syrup

1/2 c. peanut butter
1 t. vanilla
1/3 c. semi-sweet
    chocolate chips

Combine oats and margarine and microwave about 5 minutes on high, stirring twice. Stir in sugar, syrup, 1/4 cup peanut butter, vanilla and oat mixture in a saucepan and cook until sugar is dissolved. Continue to stir while cooking. Pour into greased 10"x6" glass baking dish. Press evenly into dish with a fork. Sprinkle chocolate chips over warm bars; let stand 5 minutes. Stir 1/4 cup peanut butter and drop by teaspoons onto warm bars. Let soften a minute. Spread with back of spoon, mixing with chips for a marbled effect.

Peanut Butter Yummies

A no-bake recipe kids love.

3 c. powdered sugar
1/4 c. brown sugar, packed

1/2 c. margarine, softened
2 c. peanut butter, smooth

With rotary mixer, beat all ingredients well. Pat into a 15-1/2"x10-1/2" jelly roll pan. Roll flat on top with a rolling pin.

Topping:

Melt 2 cups semi-sweet chocolate chips and one tablespoon margarine in top of double boiler. Spread over the top and cut into squares. Makes about 36.

> Save the arrival of Christmas cards for opening at suppertime so everyone can see.

White Chocolate Cake

This triple-layer cake is elegant and different!

1 c. butter
2 c. sugar
4 eggs, beaten
4 oz. white chocolate, melted
2-1/2 c. flour

1 t. baking powder
1 t. vanilla
1 c. buttermilk
1 c. pecans or walnuts, chopped
1 c. flaked coconut

Cream butter and sugar with a mixer. Add eggs and melted choco-late, blending well. Add flour, baking powder, vanilla, buttermilk, chopped nuts and coconut. Blend well and pour into 3 prepared cake pans. Bake at 350 degrees about 35 minutes.

Icing:

1/2 c. butter or
   margarine, melted
4 oz. white chocolate

6 T. buttermilk
16-oz. box powdered sugar
1 t. vanilla

Mix butter, white chocolate and buttermilk together in a sauce pan and heat gently. Remove from heat, add powdered sugar and vanilla, then return to heat to blend. Ice when cake is completely cool. Garnish with white or milk chocolate curls. For gift-giving, bake the cakes in mini-tube or bundt pans. Wrap each one in clear wrap tied with ribbon.

Macadamia Shortbread

A simple recipe for nutty shortbread.

1 c. flour
3/4 c. powdered sugar
1/4 c. cornstarch
1 c. macadamia nuts,
   finely chopped

3/4 c. butter, room temperature
24 macadamia nut halves
   (optional)
additional powdered sugar
   for garnish

Whisk dry ingredients. Stir in nuts. In another bowl, beat butter until creamy. Carefully beat in dry ingredients. Shape into balls and flatten with fork. Press a nut half into each cookie (optional). Bake at 300 degrees for 25 to 30 minutes. Sprinkle with powdered sugar if desired.

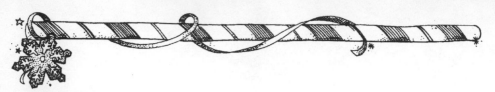

Orange Blossoms

Tiny orange-frosted cupcakes are a bite-sized treat.

2-layer yellow cake mix with
   ingredients listed on box

juice of 2 lemons
1 t. lemon rind, grated

Orange Topping:

1 t. orange rind, grated
juice of 2 oranges

3 c. powdered sugar

Prepare cake mix as directed, adding lemon juice and rind to mix, and bake in small muffin tins. While cakes are baking, mix topping ingredients together. When you remove the tiny cupcakes from the oven, dip them into the orange topping. Put on wax paper until completely cool, then serve on a doily-lined platter garnished with orange wheels.

Texas Sheet Cake

Everyone loves this big, rich, chocolate cake.

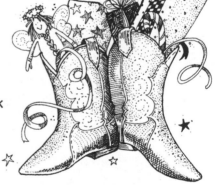

4 rounded T. cocoa
1/2 c. butter
1/2 c. oil
1 c. water
2 c. flour
2 c. sugar

2 eggs
1/2 c. buttermilk
1 t. baking soda
1/2 t. salt
1 t. vanilla

Combine cocoa, butter, oil and water in a saucepan and bring to a boil; remove from heat. Blend flour and sugar in a large bowl. Add butter mixture, eggs, buttermilk, soda, salt, vanilla and blend well. Grease and flour a large sheet pan (jelly roll pan). Bake at 400 degrees for 20 minutes. While still warm, smother in Hot Chocolate Frosting.

Hot Chocolate Frosting:

1/2 c. butter
4 T. cocoa
6 T. milk

16 oz. powdered sugar
1 t. vanilla
toasted English walnuts

Boil butter, cocoa and milk in a saucepan. Add sugar, vanilla and walnuts. Pour over cake while it's still hot.

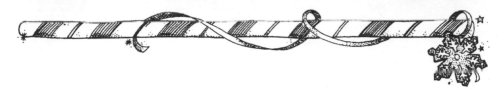

Almond Tea Cakes

When you want to serve a sweet little something.

1 c. butter
1-1/4 c. sugar
4 eggs
1 c. flour
1 t. baking powder

1 t. salt
4 t. vanilla
1/2 t. almond extract
14 to 16 oz. almonds,
    chopped well

Cream butter and sugar with an electric mixer. Add eggs and mix well; then mix in remaining ingredients by hand. Bake in mini-muffin pans at 350 degrees 10 to 15 minutes, or until done.

Makes 24.

Caramel Corn

Great for slumber parties or whenever you have a houseful of munchers!

1/2 c. margarine
2 c. brown sugar
1/2 c. light sweet
  corn syrup

1/2 t. salt
1 t. vanilla
1 t. baking soda
6 qts. popped popcorn

Heat margarine, brown sugar, sweet corn syrup and salt until it comes to a boil. Continue to boil for 5 minutes without stirring. Remove from heat. Add vanilla and soda. Stir. Pour over 6 quarts of freshly popped popcorn. Bake one hour at 250 degrees, stirring every 20 minutes.

Paper Bag Cherry Pie

No mess, no cleanup...just delicious pie!

4 cans tart cherries, drained
1/2 t. almond extract
1-1/2 c. sugar

1/3 c. flour
2 T. butter
2 10" prepared pie crusts

In a bowl, stir together cherries, almond extract, sugar and flour. Pour into a 10-inch pie crust. Dot with butter. Top with another crust and form a small log or roll around the edge of the crust with your fingers. Snip the edge with scissors or a knife. Cut vents in a pretty pattern on top of the pie. Sprinkle with sugar. Bake in a brown paper bag at 425 degrees for one hour.

Mexican Fruit Pies

Try these for a quick brunch dessert.

6 small pre-made
flour tortillas
32-oz. can apple, cherry,
or peach pie filling

3 T. vegetable oil
powdered sugar

Soften flour tortillas for about 10 seconds in the microwave. Place 2 tablespoons pie filling in the center of each tortilla. Fold the sides over, and then close the ends. Place seam side down in a frying pan coated with hot oil. Fry over medium-high heat until golden, turning once. Drain on paper towels. Dust with powdered sugar.

Makes 6.

Ornaments can be stored inside a locking plastic bag. Leave a little air in the bag when you seal it and you will provide a cushion for the ornament. Don't blow into the bag however; this creates moisture which may damage the ornament.

Christmas Cane Cookies

So much fun for the little ones.

1 tube refrigerated sugar cookie dough
red food coloring

Divide the prepared cookie dough into two halves. Add red food coloring to one portion, mixing the color in well. Roll the dough into long, narrow strips. Twist a red strip together with a white one and round the top to make a candy cane. Bake on a greased cookie sheet according to directions. Sprinkle with red sugar crystals while still hot.

Chocolate Crinkles

Put some crinkles 'n milk out for Kris Kringle on Christmas Eve!

4 oz. unsweetened chocolate	**2 c. flour**
1/2 c. shortening	**2 t. baking powder**
2 c. sugar	**1/2 t. salt**
2 t. vanilla	**1 c. chocolate chips**
4 eggs	**1 c. powdered sugar, sifted**

Melt chocolate and shortening in a double boiler over hot water. Stir in sugar. Place in a medium bowl and cool. Beat until blended. Add vanilla. Beat in eggs one at a time, mixing well after each. In another medium bowl, sift flour, baking powder and salt. Stir into chocolate mixture. Stir in chips. Refrigerate several hours. Break off small pieces and form into one-inch balls. Roll balls in powdered sugar and bake 10 minutes at 375 degrees. Place on racks to cool.

Makes approximately 70.

Fun 'n Simple Sheet Cake

A great way to dress up a boxed cake mix.

1 pkg. Swiss chocolate or
   regular chocolate cake mix
4 large eggs
3/4 c. oil
3/4 c. water

1 small pkg. instant coconut
   or vanilla pudding mix
1/4 c. granulated sugar
walnuts or pecans, chopped
1 large bag milk chocolate chips

Spray jelly roll pan (including sides) with a non-stick spray. Beat cake mix, eggs, oil, water and pudding for two minutes, getting out lumps. Pour in the pan and sprinkle sugar over top. Now sprinkle walnuts or pecans over the top along with the chocolate chips. Bake in a hot oven at 350 degrees for 22 to 25 minutes.

Swedish Pancakes

Kids love jam roll-ups...spread with cream cheese and strawberry jam, then roll them up!

1-1/4 c. biscuit mix
2 c. milk

3 eggs
1/4 c. butter or margarine, melted

Sides:
   sour cream
   apricot syrup
   maple syrup

   peanut butter
   applesauce

Whisk together mix, milk and eggs. Pour batter onto greased griddle, turning when brown. Remove to a warm platter. Serve with sour cream and apricot syrup or lightly cover with peanut butter, then applesauce and hot maple syrup.

Makes 12 to 14 pancakes.

Vanilla Wafers

Serve alongside steaming mugs of hot cocoa.

1 c. sugar
1/2 c. margarine
1 t. vanilla
1 large egg

1-1/3 c. flour
1/4 t. baking powder
1/4 t. salt

Combine sugar and margarine in a mixing bowl; beat well. Add vanilla and egg; mix. Add remaining dry ingredients; mix well. Drop by heaping teaspoonfuls onto a greased baking sheet. Bake at 350 degrees for 10 to 12 minutes.

Makes 24.

Raisin Bread

An easy quick bread for breakfast or a snack.

1 c. sugar
1/2 t. salt
3-1/4 c. flour
1 T. baking powder

1 egg, beaten
1-1/2 c. milk
1 c. raisins

Mix dry ingredients. Stir in beaten egg and milk just until blended. Fold in raisins. Bake in a greased 9"x5" loaf pan. Bake at 325 degrees for 60 to 70 minutes.

Scrumptious breads

When traveling with small children, have tiny inexpensive pre-Christmas presents to give them along the way. It helps to keep them occupied. If the children are old enough, give them a map and tell them in which towns or cities they will receive surprises. They'll have fun keeping track.

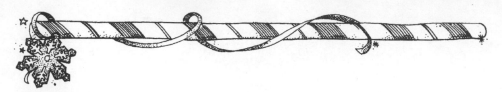

Judy's Prize-Winning Toasted Pecan Cake

This local winner was featured on the front page of the San Diego newspaper.

1-1/3 c. toasted pecans, chopped
1/4 c. butter
3 c. flour
2 t. baking powder
1/2 t. salt

1 c. butter, softened
2 c. sugar
4 large eggs
1 c. milk
2 t. vanilla

Toast pecans in 1/4 cup butter in 350 degree oven for 20 to 25 minutes. Stir frequently. Sift flour with baking powder and salt. Cream one cup butter. Gradually add sugar to butter, creaming well. Blend in eggs. Add dry ingredients, alternating with milk. Beat well after each addition. Stir in vanilla extract and toasted pecans. Pour batter into three 8 or 9-inch greased and floured cake pans. Bake at 350 degrees for 20 to 25 minutes or until a toothpick inserted in the center comes out clean. Cool before frosting.

Frosting:

2/3 c. toasted pecans, chopped
1/4 c. butter
1 lb. powdered sugar
1 t. vanilla
4 or 6 T. evaporated milk

Blend all ingredients except pecans with rotary beater. Stir in pecans. Frost cake.

A joy that's shared is a joy made double!

English Proverb

140

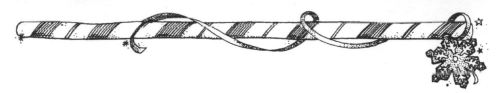

German Sweet Choco-Nut Pie

Better than a pudding pie!

1/4 c. butter or margarine,
   melted
1/2 c. pecans, chopped
2 c. coconut, flaked
4 oz. sweet baking chocolate

2 c. mini-marshmallows
1/2 c. milk
1 T. instant coffee crystals
8-oz. tub frozen whipped
   topping

Combine butter, nuts, and coconut and press into bottom and sides of 9-inch pie pan. Bake at 325 degrees for 15 to 20 minutes. Cool. Heat chocolate, mini marshmallows, milk, and coffee over low heat, stirring constantly until smooth and melted. Chill until slightly thickened. Fold in whipped topping. Pour into crust and chill. Garnish with whipped topping and chocolate curls.

Double Chocolate Sheet Cake

This chocolatey rich cake is baked with the topping already in place.

1 pkg. white cake mix
1 large pkg. chocolate
   pudding mix
4 large eggs
3/4 c. oil
3/4 c. water

1 c. walnuts, chopped
1/4 c. sugar
1 t. cinnamon
1 large bag milk chocolate
   pieces

Beat first 5 ingredients together with mixer. Pour into large cookie sheet or jelly roll pan sprayed with non-stick spray. Sprinkle top with walnuts. Blend sugar and cinnamon and sprinkle over nuts. Sprinkle on milk chocolate pieces. Press entire cake lightly with hand. Bake at 350 degrees for 25 minutes.

Cranberry Bread

Fresh cranberry bread for your turkey dinner.

2 c. flour
1 c. sugar
1-1/2 t. baking powder
1/2 t. soda
1 t. salt
juice and zest of 1 orange

2 T. shortening
boiling water
1 large egg, beaten
1 c. walnuts, chopped
1 c. raw cranberries, halved

Sift dry ingredients together. Combine juice, zest and shortening with enough boiling water to yield a total of 3/4 cup. Cool slightly and add beaten egg. Blend liquid ingredients in with the dry ingredients, stirring only until flour mixture is dampened. Blend in walnuts and cranberries. Pour into two sprayed loaf pans. Bake at 350 degrees until done.

Cranberry Glaze for Cheesecake

A quick red glaze for the cheesecake on the next page.

16-oz. can whole cranberry sauce
1 T. cornstarch
1 T. cold water
red food coloring

Heat berries in a saucepan. Dissolve corn starch in water and stir into berries. Cook until thickened. Spoon over cheesecake. Chill.

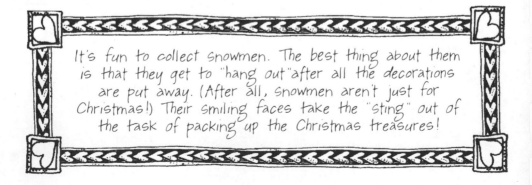

It's fun to collect snowmen. The best thing about them is that they get to "hang out" after all the decorations are put away. (After all, snowmen aren't just for Christmas!) Their smiling faces take the "sting" out of the task of packing up the Christmas treasures!

One of the Best Cheesecakes
Some say it's the very best!

1 c. graham cracker crumbs
2 T. sugar
1/4 t. cinnamon
3 T. margarine, melted
16 oz. cream cheese,
   softened

3/4 c. sugar
1 t. lemon extract or
   1 T. lemon juice
dash of lemon rind
1/2 t. vanilla
2 large eggs, beaten

Topping:

1 c. sour cream   3 T. sugar   1/2 t. vanilla

Mix first 4 ingredients and press into a 9-inch spring-form pan. Bake 10 minutes at 325 degrees. Mix remaining ingredients together for filling. Pour into crust and bake at 325 degrees for 30 minutes. Mix together topping ingredients and pour over cake. Bake another 7 minutes at 325 degrees. Serve chilled with Cranberry Glaze.

Save A piece for Santa!

143

In the childhood memories
of every good cook,
There's a large kitchen,
A warm stove,
A simmering pot and a mom.

Barbara Costikyan

Holiday Gift Cakes

Make them as big or little as you want, and decorate
accordingly. Wrap in brown paper tied with homespun
or paper twist and a sprig of pine or holly.

8-oz. pkg. cream cheese,
   softened
1 c. (2 sticks) margarine,
   softened
1-1/2 c. granulated sugar
1-1/2 t. vanilla
4 eggs

2-1/4 c. sifted cake flour, divided
1-1/2 t. baking powder
3/4 c. maraschino cherries
   (one 8-oz. jar) well-drained,
   chopped
1 c. pecans, chopped and divided

Glaze:

1-1/2 c. confectioners'
   sugar, sifted
2 T. milk

red or green maraschino
   cherries and pecan halves
   for decoration

Thoroughly blend softened cream cheese, margarine, sugar and
vanilla. Add eggs, one at a time, mixing well after each addition.
Sift 2 cups flour with baking powder. Gradually add sifted flour
mixture to batter. Dredge cherries and 1/2 cup pecans with remaining
1/4 cup flour; fold into batter. Grease a 10-inch bundt or tube pan;
sprinkle with 1/2 cup finely chopped pecans. Pour batter into pan. Bake
in a preheated 325 degree oven one hour and 20 minutes, or until
done. Cool 5 minutes; remove from pan. While cake is baking, prepare
glaze; combine confectioners' sugar and milk. Add more milk, if needed,
for drizzling consistency. Drizzle glaze over top and sides of cake.
Decorate with cherries and pecan halves, as desired.

Yield: One 10-inch cake.

Variations

For Christmas gifts, bake the cakes in oven-proof cans or other containers and omit the 1/2 cup finely chopped nuts for lining pans.

Pour 2 cups batter into each of three greased one-pound coffee cans. Bake in a 325 degree oven one hour.

Pour 1/2 cup batter into each of 11 greased 8-ounce tomato sauce cans. Bake in a 325 degree oven 25 minutes.

Pour one cup batter into each of 5 greased 6"x3-1/2" loaf pans. Bake in a 325 degree oven 45 to 50 minutes.

Duck Creek Cranberry Bread

Perfect for a Christmas tea.

2 sticks butter
2 c. sugar
4 eggs
1/2 c. evaporated milk

1 t. vanilla
2 c. flour
1 c. raw cranberries, chopped
1 c. pecans, chopped

In a large bowl, cream butter and sugar at medium speed until light and fluffy. Add eggs one a time. Add milk, vanilla, and flour one ingredient at a time and beat at low speed until blended, constantly scraping bowl. Fold in chopped cranberries and nuts. Bake at 325 degrees in a tube pan until light brown, approximately 50 to 60 minutes.

Apricot Coriander Pecan Bread

A delicious addition to Christmas brunch.

1/4 c. butter or
    margarine, softened
1-1/4 c. sugar
1 egg, beaten
2 c. all-purpose flour, sifted
1/2 t. baking powder
1/2 t. baking soda
1/2 t. salt

1 T. coriander, ground
1 c. canned apricots,
    mashed and drained
2 T. sour cream
1/2 t. almond extract
1/2 c. pecans, chopped
1/2 c. maraschino
    cherries, halved

Grease and flour loaf pan. Beat butter and sugar in large bowl and stir in egg. Mix sifted flour, baking powder, baking soda, salt, and coriander on a piece of wax paper. Stir into sugar mixture. Fold in apricots, sour cream, and almond extract. Stir in pecans and cherries. Turn into the prepared pan. Bake 350 degrees for 50 minutes. Cool for 5 minutes. Remove from pan and cool completely. Wrap in foil or plastic wrap. Refrigerate. Allow flavors to blend for 24 hours before serving.

Gingerbread Babies

Tuck them into a little basket and leave them on someone's doorstep...surely you know someone who will give them a good home at Christmas!

1/2 c. butter softened
3/4 c. brown sugar, firmly packed
1 large egg
1/4 c. dark molasses
2-2/3 c. flour
2 t. ginger
1/2 t. nutmeg
1/2 t. cinnamon
1/2 t. allspice
1/4 t. salt

Preheat oven to 350 degrees. In mixing bowl, combine butter and brown sugar until fluffy. Add egg and molasses. In separate bowl, stir together the dry ingredients. Gradually stir dry ingredients into the butter mixture. Turn dough out onto well-floured board and roll out to 1/8-inch thickness. Cut out lots of gingerbread babies and bake on a well-greased cookie sheet for 9 to 10 minutes.

Makes 18 large gingerbread men or 50 babies.

Strawberry Hill Sweet Bread

A holiday specialty!

2 c. milk
1 stick sweet butter
1/2 to 3/4 c. warm water
1 T. white sugar
2 pkgs. dry yeast
3 large eggs, beaten
cinnamon to taste

1 t. almond extract
1 t. vanilla extract
1 c. brown sugar
up to 5 lbs. bread flour
  (can be a combination of
  white & wheat or rye)
1 egg white

Scald milk and remove from stove. Drop butter into milk and let sit until it melts and is warm, not hot. Add sugar to water. Stir until melted. Add yeast. Set aside until it foams. Add a sprinkle of cinnamon, the almond extract, vanilla extract, and brown sugar to beaten eggs. Whisk together until thick and the sugar is all wet. In a large bowl, add the warm (not hot) milk mixture. Add the egg mixture and beat with a whisk. Next add the yeast mixture; it should be foamy now. If the milk mixture is too hot, it will kill the yeast. Whisk it all together and begin to add flour. Keep adding flour until you have a nice smooth dough. Put on a floured surface and knead about 10 minutes or less, until you form a nice smooth ball. (Depending on the weather, it can take as much as 5 lbs. of flour). Then put into a large oiled bowl, turn once and put in a warm place to rise. About an hour later, punch down and let rise again. Then take out your dough.

⋆ Now the fun begins! ⋆

You can separate the dough and put it into greased loaf pans or make braids. Add raisins, more cinnamon, and roll so you have a swirl. Another option is to put the dough into greased coffee cans about half full. Using a coffee can, the bread will come out looking like a mushroom and you'll only be able to use one oven rack. Let rise about an hour longer. After it has risen, bake at 325 degrees for about 40 minutes, depending on the size of the loaves. When the bread is browned and sounds

hollow when tapped, paint a little egg white on top. Five minutes later, remove to a terry towel. If baking loaves, cool on their sides. ✦ ☆ ✦
Note: If you use coffee cans and the bread won't come out, carefully remove the bottom of the coffee can with a hand can opener and push it out the top. You will then have round slices when you cut it. Another option...buy new clay flowerpot bakers ☆. (especially made for the oven...ordinary clay pots may have some lead content), line with foil, and grease. Put a ball of dough in and let rise. When dough is close to the top, place the flower pot on a sturdy cookie sheet and bake. Leave in pot and put in an artificial piece of holly when cooled. Cover with plastic wrap and tie with a bow.

Apple Syrup

Rewarm in the microwave and serve over pancakes, French toast, or vanilla ice cream.

1 c. unsweetened apple juice　　**1/4 c. apple liqueur**
1 c. sugar　　**1 cinnamon stick**

Combine all ingredients in a saucepan over medium heat. Bring to a boil, stirring constantly, and boil for about 15 minutes or until slightly thickened. Remove from heat and pour, including the cinnamon stick, into a sterilized 12-ounce bottle. Cap tightly and refrigerate.

For less stress and more time to really enjoy the holidays, bake early and freeze the goodies. Months later what a sweet treat to find cookies that were forgotten or overlooked.

Christmas Morning Almond Pound Cake

Serve while the presents are being opened, or make it as a gift for a family you love.

2/3 c. butter, softened
8 oz. almond paste
1 t. almond extract
1 t. vanilla extract
1-1/4 c. white sugar
4 large eggs

1 t. baking powder
1/4 c. sour cream
2-1/2 c. white flour, sifted
1/2 to 3/4 c. milk
powdered sugar for topping

Preheat oven to 325 degrees. Grease and flour a bundt or tube pan and set aside. In a bowl, beat together the softened butter, almond paste, and extracts until smooth. Slowly add the sugar and beat again, then add the eggs one at a time, beating after each addition. Add the baking powder to the sour cream, beat together and add to the above mixture. Slowly add the flour alternately with the milk until you have a nice smooth batter. Pour into prepared pan and bake at 325 degrees for 45 to 60 minutes, or until the top is golden brown and it springs back when touched. Turn off oven and open oven door. Let sit about 1/2 hour and then remove to counter on rack or cutting board. When cool, remove to a special dish. Before serving, sprinkle with powdered sugar and top with maraschino cherry halves, or make a glaze with powdered sugar and milk and drizzle over the cake. This can also be served with ice cream or with whipped cream as a dessert.

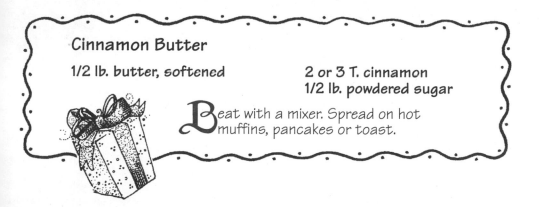

Cinnamon Butter

1/2 lb. butter, softened

2 or 3 T. cinnamon
1/2 lb. powdered sugar

Beat with a mixer. Spread on hot muffins, pancakes or toast.

Cranberry Walnut Apple Bread

Try using half a loaf of this bread to substitute for half of your regular bread in your stuffing recipe. They'll be coming back for thirds...but no leftover stuffing for the next day!

2 c. apples, cored, peeled, and finely chopped
3/4 c. sugar
2 T. oil
1 large egg
1-1/2 c. all-purpose flour

1-1/2 t. baking powder
1/2 t. baking soda
1 t. cinnamon
1 c. cranberries, fresh or frozen
1/2 c. walnuts, chopped

Preheat oven to 350. Grease and flour a loaf pan. Combine apples, sugar, and oil in a medium mixing bowl. Add the egg, mixing well. Combine dry ingredients in a separate bowl. Add to the apple mixture, mixing until the dry ingredients are moist. Stir in the cranberries and the walnuts. Spread batter evenly into a prepared loaf pan. Bake one hour, or until a toothpick inserted comes out clean.

Makes one loaf.

Apricot Nut Bread

Wrap it up for your favorite hostess.

2-1/4 c. biscuit mix
1 c. oats
3/4 c. sugar
1 t. baking powder
1/4 t. salt

1/2 c. dried apricots, snipped
1 c. walnuts, chopped
1-1/4 c. milk
1 egg, lightly beaten

Combine dry ingredients in a bowl. Add fruit and nuts and mix to coat. Add remaining milk and egg, and stir just to moisten. Pour into a 9"x5"x3" loaf pan sprayed with nonstick spray. Bake for one hour at 350 degrees. Test with a toothpick for doneness.

Coconut Oatmeal Cookies

A really different, crunchy-chewy coconut-lover's treat!

1/2 c. flour
1/2 t. baking powder
1/2 t. salt
1/2 t. baking soda
1 c. coconut, shredded
1 c. quick-cooking oatmeal

1/2 c. almonds, chopped
1/4 lb. butter
1/2 c. white sugar
1/2 c. brown sugar
1 egg
1 t. vanilla

Preheat oven to 350 degrees and grease baking sheets. Sift flour and then resift with baking powder and salt. Dissolve soda in one teaspoon of tepid water. Measure coconut, oatmeal, and almonds. Soften butter with hands and cream with the sugars to a fluffy mixture. Add unbeaten egg. Blend well. Add flour mixture, dissolved soda and vanilla. Oatmeal, coconut, and almonds are added last, and dough will seem pretty hard. Shape little balls with hands or drop by spoon onto greased cookie sheet 3 inches apart. Bake 10 to 12 minutes.

Makes 75 cookies.

Eggnog Cakes

Drizzle these little cakes with a mixture of orange juice and powdered sugar.

1/2 c. walnuts or pecans,
   finely chopped
18-1/4 oz. pkg. yellow cake mix
1 c. eggnog, refrigerated

1/4 c. vegetable oil
3 large eggs
2 T. orange juice
1/4 t. ground nutmeg

Generously grease and flour 12 individual-sized (one-cup) bundt pans or one 10-inch (12-cup) bundt pan. Sprinkle nuts in bottom of prepared pans (about 2 teaspoons in each individual pan). Heat oven to 350 degrees for individual-sized pans or 325 degrees for 10-inch pan. In large bowl, with electric mixer at low speed, combine dry cake mix, eggnog, oil, eggs, orange juice, and nutmeg; beat 2 minutes. Pour batter into prepared pans, filling each pan half full. Bake individual cakes 20 to 25 minutes or 10-inch cake one hour, or until cake tester inserted in center comes out clean. Cool in pan on wire rack 15 minutes. Remove cakes from pans to wire rack to cool completely. Store cakes in an airtight container. Note: If baking individual cakes in batches, be sure to wipe pans clean with paper towels and generously grease and flour again before reusing.

Pecan Candy Rolls

A really different Christmas candy.

1 t. vanilla
1/4 t. almond extract
7-1/2 oz. jar of
   marshmallow cream
3-1/2 c. powdered sugar

1-1/2 lbs. caramels
2 T. water
1 lb. pecans or peanuts,
   broken and chopped

Mix extracts with marshmallow cream. Add powdered sugar and knead well, using your hands to form six small rolls. Dip rolls in melted caramel and roll in pecans or peanuts. Chill and wrap in plastic wrap.

Christmas Truffles

Will last up to a month in the refrigerator, unless your family finds them. Then they'll last only a day or two!

2/3 c. heavy cream
12 oz. good quality
   chocolate chips
4 T. unsalted butter,
   room temperature
mini cupcake papers
   (found in specialty
   stores just for candy)

Optional (for coating):
   coconut
   ground nuts
   powdered sugar
   chocolate sprinkles
   cocoa powder

In a heavy saucepan, heat cream until just coming to a boil. Remove from heat and whisk in the chocolate chips and the butter. Beat until smooth. Pour this into a glass dish and place plastic wrap directly on the chocolate mixture. Refrigerate for about 3 hours. Then, working with clean hands or plastic gloves, take a spoonful of chocolate and roll it between your palms. Dip the ball into cocoa powder, coconut, etc. and place in a mini cupcake paper or on a sheet of wax paper. Place in an airtight container and refrigerate.

We wish you a Merry Christmas and a happy New Year; a pocket full of money and a house full of cheer; and a great fat pig to last you all the year.

Traditional song

Holiday Chocolate Bars

Cut these bars small – they are very rich.

1-3/4 c. unsifted flour
1/2 c. sugar
1/4 c. cocoa
1/2 c. cold margarine
   or butter
1 egg, beaten

14-oz. can sweetened
   condensed milk
12-oz. pkg. semi-sweet
   chocolate chips
1 c. chopped nuts

Preheat oven to 350 degrees. Combine flour, sugar, and cocoa; cut in margarine until crumbly. Add egg. Mix until well blended. Reserve 1-1/2 cups crumb mixture. Press remainder evenly on bottom of greased 13"x9" baking pan. Bake 10 minutes. In saucepan, combine the sweetened condensed milk and one cup of chocolate chips. Cook over low heat and stir until chips melt and mixture is smooth. Spread evenly over prepared crust. Add nuts and remaining chocolate chips to reserved crumb mixture and sprinkle evenly over top. Bake 25 to 30 minutes until center is set. Cool and cut into bars. Store covered at room temperature.

Orange Butter

1 lb. butter, softened
juice of 4 oranges
1 T. orange rind, grated
1/2 lb. powered sugar

Blend and chill. Yummy on muffins, cornbread or waffles.

Mini Christmas Cheesecakes

Look so pretty on your dessert table.

3 8-oz. pkgs. cream
   cheese, softened
1 c. sugar

5 eggs
1-1/2 t. vanilla

Mix together cream cheese and sugar. Add eggs one at a time. Add vanilla and mix again. Pour into mini foil cups, filling 3/4 full. Bake 20 minutes at 350 degrees. Remove from oven and let stand 5 minutes.

Makes 36 mini-cakes.

Topping:

1 c. sour cream
1/2 c. sugar

2 cans cherry pie filling
36 cherries set aside for garnish

Blend topping ingredients by hand. Top each mini-cake with 1/2 teaspoon of the mixture and return to the oven for 5 minutes. When cooled, top each cheesecake with one nice red cherry, a little of the juice around it. Keep refrigerated.

Christmas Peppermint Candy

The children really love this candy, and it's so pretty too. It's quite easy and can be started and finished in 30 minutes max!

2 pkgs. of white vanilla bark
2 jumbo candy canes

(If using the thin candy canes, you'll need 15 to 20)

Melt the vanilla bark in the microwave on low power, stirring half way through. While melting, put the candy canes in a locking plastic baggie and smash with a hammer into little pieces. When the bark is smooth and melted, add the peppermint chips and stir until covered. Pour the mixture out onto a large piece of aluminum foil and, with a spatula, spread the mixture out thin. Allow to harden, pull aluminum foil off and break into bite-sized pieces. Put in an airtight container, and it lasts forever!

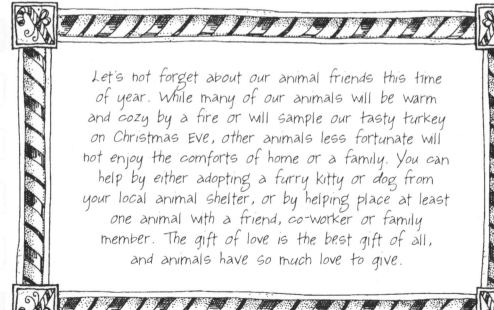

Let's not forget about our animal friends this time of year. While many of our animals will be warm and cozy by a fire or will sample our tasty turkey on Christmas Eve, other animals less fortunate will not enjoy the comforts of home or a family. You can help by either adopting a furry kitty or dog from your local animal shelter, or by helping place at least one animal with a friend, co-worker or family member. The gift of love is the best gift of all, and animals have so much love to give.

Moravian Sugar Cookies

The secret to these cookies is the buttermilk. Double or triple this one; they freeze really well!

1/2 c. margarine
1/2 c. shortening
1 c. sugar
1 c. brown sugar
2 eggs

1 t. vanilla
pinch of salt
1/2 t. soda
2 T. buttermilk
3-1/2 to 4-1/2 c. flour

Cream margarine and shortening with sugar and brown sugar. Add eggs and mix well. Add vanilla and salt. In a small cup, add baking soda to buttermilk. Let sit one minute and then add to the mixture. Add the flour and mix well. Chill up to 2 hours. Roll dough out to desired thickness and use cutters in all shapes. Bake at 375 degrees for 5 to 7 minutes ONLY. Do not overbake or expect them to turn brown. They will melt in your mouth.

Gingerbread Cookies

Triple this recipe to make 3 to 4 dozen gingerbread men... invite the kids to help decorate!

2/3 c. butter, melted
2 c. flour
   (more if making cut-outs)
1 egg
1/4 c. molasses
1 c. sugar

2 t. baking soda
1-1/2 t. cinnamon
1/2 t. ginger
1/2 t. cloves
1/2 t. salt

Mix all ingredients. Roll into one-inch balls. Roll balls in sugar. Place on lightly sprayed cookie sheet. Bake at 350 degrees for 8 minutes. Yield: Approximately 3 dozen cookies. For gingerbread men: Add enough flour to be able to roll dough. Use a well floured board. Makes 12 to 15. Men will grow in the oven.

Chocolate Surprises

You can also roll these truffle-like candies in sweet cocoa powder or grated coconut.

6-oz. pkg. semi-sweet
   chocolate pieces
1/2 c. sour cream
salt
1 c. vanilla wafer crumbs
   (about 24 vanilla wafers
   crushed with rolling pin)
2-1/2 T. rum

3 T. butter, melted
2 T. unsweetened cocoa
1/2 c. powdered sugar
1/2 c. pecans or walnuts,
   finely chopped
2-3/4 oz. jar
   chocolate sprinkles

Melt chocolate pieces in top of double boiler, over hot, not boiling water. Remove from heat, and stir in sour cream and dash of salt. Refrigerate overnight. In small bowl, mix vanilla wafer crumbs with rum, butter, cocoa, powdered sugar, chopped nuts, and a dash of salt with a fork until mixture holds its shape easily. Form chilled chocolate mixture into balls the size of a grape. Cover each chocolate ball with some of the wafer-crumb mixture. At this point, they are the size of a walnut. Roll each in chocolate sprinkles. Store in an airtight container in refrigerator for 24 hours to mellow.

Makes 2 to 2-1/2 dozen.

One of our friends from Maine taught us something new this year...she packs her gift shipments with pine cones. They're much better than styrofoam or wadded-up plastic shopping bags...not only do they protect your gifts, but they look Christmasy, can be re-used as decorations, and they're better for the environment. Make sure they're dry and opened, so no sap is running.

Chocolate Crème Fraiche Walnut Fudge

Make the crème fraiche ahead of time...it's worth it!

3 oz. unsweetened chocolate
3 c. granulated sugar
1/8 t. cream of tartar
1 c. crème fraiche
   (recipe on next page)

1/8 t. salt
1-1/2 t. vanilla
1/2 c. walnuts or pecans,
   coarsely chopped

In a heavy 3-quart saucepan, melt baking chocolate over lowest possible heat. Watch carefully! When chocolate is just melted, remove from heat. Stir in sugar and cream of tartar, mixing well and stirring up all melted chocolate from bottom of pan. Gradually stir in crème fraiche and when well combined, return pan to stove and cook and stir over medium low heat until sugar is dissolved. Stop stirring when mixture starts to boil. Cover pan briefly to wash down any sugar crystals from sides of pan. Do not leave this for even a minute, or mixture will boil over! Remove lid, put candy themometer in pan and cook to 235 degrees without stirring. All this usually happens rather quickly. Remove pan from heat. When bubbles start to subside, pour mixture slowly and carefully onto a buttered marble slab or simply set pan away from heat to a cool surface and allow temperature to cool to 110 degrees. If you have poured candy onto a marble slab, let it cool until you can lightly touch it and mixture is barely warm. Stir fudge in pan or work candy on marble with a wide spatula until candy starts to lose its gloss and thicken. Quickly stir in salt, vanilla, and nuts, and pour into small buttered tins or an 8-inch square baking pan. (Smaller pans make thicker fudge.) When cool, cut into squares if desired. It's best to let it sit overnight before cutting and eating.

Crème Fraiche (from left)

To make walnut fudge even better.

1 c. heavy whipping cream　　　**2 T. cultured buttermilk**

Put the whipping cream in a sterile one-pint jar, setting the lid aside. Place jar of whipping cream, uncovered, in the microwave. Heat 20 to 40 seconds on high, or to 85 degrees. If temperature goes a bit higher, cool cream to 85 degrees. Stir in buttermilk and blend well. Cover top of jar with plastic wrap, secure wrap with a rubber band and poke a few holes in the plastic with a toothpick. Set in a warm place or leave at room temperature until mixture thickens. This will take from 12 to 28 hours, depending on surrounding temperature. Stir mixture well, place lid over plastic wrap, and keep refrigerated until ready to use.

Cranberry Treasure Cookies

You'll love this "berried" treasure!

1-2/3 c. all-purpose flour
1 t. baking soda
1/2 t. salt
1/2 c. (1 stick) butter
　　or margarine, softened
3/4 c. brown sugar,
　　firmly packed

1 egg
10-oz. pkg. (1-1/2 c.) white
　　chocolate baking pieces
1 c. cranberries, rinsed
　　and patted dry
1/2 c. pecans, coarsely chopped
1 t. grated orange rind

Preheat oven to 375 degrees. Grease two large cookie sheets. In a small bowl, combine flour, baking soda and salt; set aside. In a large mixing bowl, beat butter and brown sugar until creamy. Blend in egg. Gradually beat in flour mixture. Stir in white chocolate, cranberries, pecans and orange rind. Drop by heaping tablespoons onto prepared cookie sheet. Bake 12 to 14 minutes until golden brown. Let stand 2 minutes. Remove from cookie sheets; cool. Store loosely covered, up to 3 days.

White Chocolate Fudge

Try this recipe using almonds or macadamia nuts, too.

2 c. sugar
3/4 c. sour cream
1/2 c. margarine
12 oz. white chocolate,
    coarsely chopped

7-oz. jar marshmallow cream
3/4 c. walnuts, chopped
3/4 c. dried apricots, chopped

Combine sugar, sour cream and margarine in heavy 2-1/2 to 3-quart saucepan; bring to full rolling boil stirring constantly. Continue boiling 7 minutes over medium heat or until candy thermometer reaches 234 degrees, stirring constantly to prevent scorching. Remove from heat; stir in chocolate until melted. Add remaining ingredients; beat until well blended. Pour into greased 8 or 9-inch square baking pan.

Makes 2-1/2 pounds.

Brownie Mounds

*You can drizzle these with melted sweet chocolate
for an elegant look.*

3-1/2 c. flour, sifted
1 t. baking powder
1/2 t. salt
2/3 c. margarine
1-1/2 c. sugar
2/3 c. light corn syrup

2 eggs
6 1-oz. squares unsweetened
    chocolate, melted
2 t. vanilla
1-1/2 c. nuts, coarsely chopped

Sift flour, baking powder and salt. Mix margarine and sugar, then stir in corn syrup and eggs. Stir in flour, chocolate, vanilla and nuts. Drop by heaping tablespoons onto greased baking sheet. Bake in 350 degree oven 10 to 12 minutes. Do not overbake. Cookies should bake just until set.

Makes 4 dozen.

Chocolate Snowball Truffles

Your chocolate-craving friends will be delighted!

1/2 c. heavy cream
1/4 c. unsalted butter
pinch of salt
8 oz. semi-sweet or
   bittersweet chocolate,
   in pieces

1 t. vanilla
2 T. unsweetened cocoa powder
2 T. powdered sugar,
   plus extra for coating

In a saucepan, warm cream, butter, and salt over low heat until butter is melted. Stir in chocolate and reduce heat to low. Cook until chocolate is melted and smooth. Remove from heat and stir in vanilla. Pour mixture into medium bowl, cover with plastic wrap, and refrigerate until firm, about three hours. Shape and coat truffles: in a small bowl, mix together cocoa and two tablespoons powdered sugar. Place bowl of chocolate in larger bowl of ice water to keep mixture firm. Using a melon baller or two teaspoons dipped in powdered sugar, scoop some chilled chocolate into small balls. Roll ball in cocoa-sugar mixture. You can sprinkle your fingers and palms with powdered sugar and shape the mixture by hand, but you'll need to work quickly to keep the chocolate from melting. After coating each truffle, place them in the refrigerator. Let truffles stand at room temperature for 10 to 15 minutes before serving; do not let them remain at room temperature very long or they will become too soft.

When you send a boxful of gifts faraway, instead of sticking bows on the gifts, only to have them crushed in shipping, fill a locking plastic bag with bows and enough air so that it cushions the packages and the bows. The bows can be stuck on the gifts after they arrive, safe and sound.

Chocolate Mint-Wiches

Cool mint cookies with a creamy mint middle.

2/3 c. shortening
1/2 c. sugar
1 egg
6 oz. mint chocolate chips
1/4 c. sweet corn syrup

1-3/4 c. flour
2 t. soda
1/4 t. salt
50 to 60 chocolate-covered
   peppermint patties

Combine shortening, sugar and egg in a saucepan and heat while stirring. Blend in remaining ingredients (except peppermints) and stir until chocolate chips are melted. Chill in the refrigerator for 2 hours. Shape into balls about the size of a large grape. Roll in sugar. Be sure not to make balls too large, or mash them down. Bake at 350 degrees for 7 to 10 minutes, watching closely that they don't burn. Remove from the oven and immediately press a mint between two warm cookies.

Makes 50 to 60 cookie sandwiches.

Surprise a friend or a grandparent with a small child's voice on the telephone answering machine. When you know for sure they aren't home, telephone them and have your child sing "Twinkle, Twinkle Little Star," "Jingle Bells," or "Away in a Manger." These little songs should be enough to delight and lighten anyone's day.

Spiced Pecans

Set them out and watch them disappear, or box and wrap them as gifts.

1 c. sugar
1 to 2 t. ground cinnamon
1 t. salt
1/2 t. ground nutmeg

1/4 t. ground cloves
1/4 c. water
3 c. pecan halves

Combine first 6 ingredients in a large saucepan. Place over medium heat, stirring constantly until sugar dissolves; then cook to soft ball stage (about 232 degrees). Remove from heat; add pecans, stirring until well coated. Spread pecans on wax paper, and separate nuts with a fork. Cool.

Woodchucks

Deliciously crunchy!

2 c. walnuts
  (or 1 cup black walnuts
  and 1 cup pecans)
1 c. dates, pitted

1 c. brown sugar, packed
2 eggs
3-1/2 c. coconut,
  shredded and divided

Put walnuts and dates through coarse blade of grinder or chop coarsely using steel blade of food processor or blender. Add brown sugar, eggs and 1-1/2 cups coconut; mix well. Shape mixture into one-inch balls. Roll balls in remaining 2 cups coconut and place balls on well-greased baking sheet. Bake in a preheated 375 degree oven 10 to 12 minutes, or until coconut is toasted. Cookies will be soft so remove them carefully from pans. They will firm up as they cool.

Homemade Caramels

Tuck these into a little wax paper-lined box and tie
with a piece of homespun.

2 c. sugar
1/2 lb. butter

1-1/2 c. dark sweet corn syrup
1 pt. cream, divided

Place sugar, butter, corn syrup and 1/2 pint cream in a large saucepan and bring to a boil. Add remaining 1/2 pint cream, bit by bit,
never letting the syrup stop boiling until it reaches the hard ball
stage at 245 degrees. Add one teaspoon vanilla and nuts if desired.
Pour into large shallow buttered pan. When cold, cut and wrap in
wax paper.

Chocolate Chip Pudding Cookies

Try making these with different flavors of pudding.

1 c. butter
1 c. brown sugar
1 t. vanilla
2 eggs
2-1/4 c. flour

1 t. baking soda
large pkg. instant
    coconut pudding
12 oz. chocolate chips
1 c. nuts, chopped

Cream butter and sugar. Add the remaining ingredients and
combine well. Drop by heaping tablespoons onto greased
baking sheets. Bake at 375 degrees for 8 to 10 minutes.

Makes 24 large cookies.

Recycle your Christmas tree at the local park.
Have a drop-off place for all trees so they can be
ground into mulch and used again.

Pumpkin Nut Roll

Festive and flavorful. A favorite!

3 eggs
1 c. sugar
2/3 c. canned pumpkin
1 T. lemon juice
3/4 c. flour
1 t. baking powder

2 t. cinnamon
1 t. ginger
1 t. nutmeg
1/2 t. salt
1 c. walnuts or pecans,
    finely chopped

Filling:

1 c. powdered sugar
2 3-oz. pkgs. cream
    cheese, softened

4 T. butter
1/2 t. vanilla

Beat the eggs for five minutes on high speed. Gradually add sugar. Stir in pumpkin and lemon juice. In a separate bowl, mix together flour, baking powder, cinnamon, ginger, nutmeg and salt. Fold this into the pumpkin mixture. Grease a 10"x15"x1" jelly roll pan or cookie sheet, line it with wax paper, and grease the paper. Spread batter over the paper and top with the nuts. Bake 15 minutes at 375 degrees (or until done). Turn out onto a clean towel sprinkled with powdered sugar. Mix together the powdered sugar, cream cheese, butter and vanilla and spread filling over the cake. Gently roll it up as for a jelly roll, using the wax paper to help push the roll. Cool and serve chilled.

Lemon Cookies

Very cheerful and lemony.

2 large eggs
1/2 T. lemon extract
2 T. lemon juice
3 drops yellow food coloring
1 c. butter-flavored shortening
1/2 c. plus 2 T. lemon gelatin mix

1 c. sugar
2 t. cream of tartar
1 t. soda
1/2 t. salt
2-3/4 c. flour

Combine eggs, lemon extract, lemon juice, food coloring and shortening and beat well. In a separate bowl, combine gelatin, sugar, cream of tartar, soda, salt and flour. Add to egg mixture and mix well. Drop by teaspoonfuls onto greased cookie sheet. Flatten just a little with a spatula or your fingers. Sprinkle a little lemon gelatin powder over each cookie. Bake at 400 degrees just until done, about 9 minutes.

Makes about 36 to 48 cookies.

Mexican Wedding Cookies

A crunchy, classic cookie.

1 c. margarine, softened
1/4 c. powdered sugar
1 t. almond extract

2 c. flour
1/4 c. walnuts, finely chopped

Beat first three ingredients until creamy. Add flour and nuts. Chill for a couple of hours. Make small balls and bake at 375 degrees for about 17 minutes. Cool a little and toss in powdered sugar.

Party Mints

Make them in a rainbow of colors. Try flavoring some of them with spearmint, also.

3 oz. cream cheese
1 T. heavy cream
food coloring

3 drops of oil of peppermint
1 lb. powdered sugar

Combine cream cheese and cream. Add remaining ingredients. Twist or roll into a rope and cut into bite-sized pieces. Let dry. To give as a gift, wrap each mint in colored plastic wrap or foil, twisting the ends, and pack in a pretty tin.

Date and Pumpkin Loaves

Mini-loaves, fragrant with spices, make great hostess gifts.

3-1/2 c. flour
2 t. baking soda
1-1/2 t. salt
1 t. cinnamon
1 t. nutmeg
1 t. allspice
3 c. sugar

1 c. oil
4 eggs, beaten
2/3 c. water
2 c. pumpkin (1-1/2 lb. can)
1-1/4 c. pecans, chopped
1 c. dates, chopped

Combine dry ingredients and mix well. Combine wet ingredients and mix with dry ingredients. Stir in pecans and dates. Pour into three small greased loaf pans. Bake at 350 degrees for one hour. Allow to sit several hours before slicing.

Fudge Truffle Cookies

The pride of the cookie exchange!

3 4-oz. bars German sweet
 baking chocolate
2 T. butter-flavored shortening
1 t. instant coffee granules
3 eggs
1-1/4 c. sugar
1 t. vanilla

1 c. toasted pecans, chopped
6 T. flour
1 t. cinnamon
1/2 t. baking powder
1/4 t. salt
3 T. sugar

Heat chocolate and shortening until melted. Remove and add coffee. Stir until smooth. Cool. Beat eggs and sugar 3 to 4 minutes. Beat in chocolate mixture and add vanilla. On low heat, beat in pecans, flour, cinnamon, baking powder and salt. Spray cookie sheets with non-stick spray. Place rounded teaspoonfuls 2 inches apart, decorating with a pecan half on top of each on top top of each cookie. Bake 350 degrees for 8 to 10 minutes or until just set (do not overbake). Cool one or 2 minutes. Put on racks and sprinkle with sugar.

Makes 36 to 48 cookies.

Raisin Apple Bread

Wrap the bread in plastic and tie a bow around the ring to make a wreath.

3 c. flour
2-1/2 c. sugar
1-1/4 c. oil
4 large eggs, lightly beaten
1 T. and 1 t. vanilla
2 t. cinnamon
1-1/2 t. salt

1-1/2 t. baking soda
1/2 t. cloves
1/2 t. baking powder
3 c. apples, peeled and diced
2/3 to 1 c. raisins
1 c. walnuts, chopped

Beat first 10 ingredients together for about 2 minutes. Stir in apples, raisins, and nuts. Bake in 2 small ring pans at 325 degrees for 60 minutes or until toothpick comes out clean.

Vanilla Chip Cookies

Rich and yummy!

1 t. soda
1 t. salt
1 t. vanilla
2 eggs
1/2 c. butter-flavored
    shortening
1/2 c. margarine
    (soften just a little)

2-1/2 c. flour
2-1/2 c. powdered sugar
1 c. vanilla chips
1 c. walnuts, chopped
garnish: chocolate-
    covered almonds

Mix soda, salt, vanilla and eggs and beat well. Add shortening and margarine and mix well. Mix in the flour and sugar and add the vanilla chips and walnuts. Drop by teaspoonfuls onto a greased cookie sheet. Put a few chocolate-covered almonds on top of each cookie. Bake at 375 degrees until golden, about 12 minutes. (Be sure to bake cookies on a cooled cookie sheet to prevent spreading.)

Makes about 48 cookies.

Brazil Nut Loaf

Take this one to a party.

1-1/2 c. flour
1-1/2 c. sugar
1 t. baking powder
1 t. salt
8-oz. bottle of maraschino
    cherries, drained

2 lbs. dates, pitted
2 lbs. walnuts, shelled
1 lb. Brazil nuts, shelled
5 large eggs, beaten
1 t. vanilla

Sift dry ingredients and add cherries, dates and nuts. Stir to coat with flour mixture. Add eggs and vanilla. With clean hands, blend everything well. Spoon into an 8-1/2"x4-1/2"x2-1/2" greased loaf pan. Bake at 325 degrees for one hour or a bit longer. Cool.

At Christmas play and make good cheer,
For Christmas comes but once a year.

Thomas Tusser

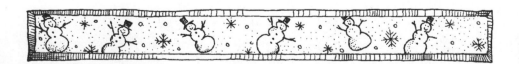

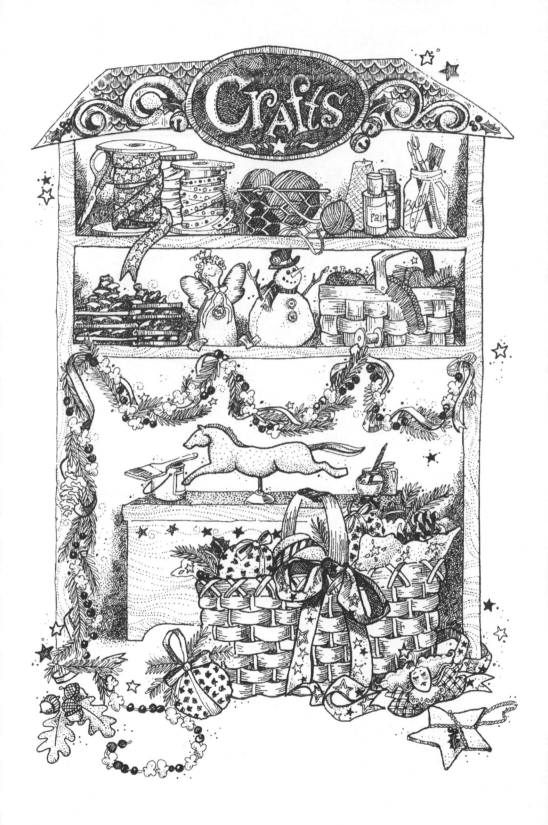

Making Merry
with creative gifts

Gingerbread House Piñata

The idea of the piñata comes from Mexico, where a hollow papier-mâché donkey is filled with toys for the children and hung from a tree. The children are blindfolded and given a stick to hit the piñata. When the piñata is finally broken, the toys fall to the ground. You can use this same idea with a gingerbread house filled with little toys for the children (or lottery tickets for adults, if you have big children in your family). On Christmas morning, let the children break it open to receive their gifts. If your gifts are a bit too large to fit inside the house, you can put gift tags inside, with the name of the child and where they must go to find their gift sacks. The gingerbread house can be made as big and fancy as you wish...complete with stained glass windows made out of melted crushed lifesavers. You can also make a simple house by putting it together with graham crackers and icing. Once you fill the house with gifts, the children can join in the fun of decorating it.

Fabric Gift Bags

Take a piece of burlap, fold it to the size you need, trim and sew up the side and bottom to resemble a sack. Sew a drawstring pocket into the top and thread it with bright red yarn. On the side of the bag, stencil a Christmas design such as a holly and Santa with acrylic paint. Tuck any gift you please inside the bag, and stuff it with mounds of bright tissue or paper shreddings. They'll be able to use the bag over and over again.

Take leftover Christmas material and make it into a small bag. Don't worry about the top; you don't have to finish it...just gather it together and tie it with ribbon. Inside the bag, fit a very tiny box of earrings or a pin. Your friends will want to save the "Christmas Bag" and use it next year for a gift they give to someone else.

Gift Tags

You may think many commercial gift tags are too small for your use. If so, you can make your own using blank 3 x 5 cards. Just fold them in half and decorate with some Christmas fabric, wrapping paper, or cut-up Christmas cards. With a little white glue, stick the picture or decoration on the front. Use a hole punch and put a hole in the corner and tie on some ribbon. The ideas are endless. Let the kids do this over the Thanksgiving holidays or on a snowy day.

★ These also make great ornaments tied onto your tree!

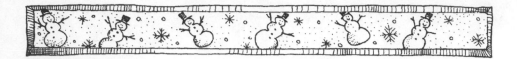

Potato-Stenciled Gift Bags

You will need:

50 brown or white lunch bags
small Christmas cookie cutters
green and red stencil paints
2 to 3 potatoes

Mom and Dad should supervise this one! Take the potatoes and slice in half. Press the cookie cutter into the half so you can see the outline. Carefully cut away the extra potato about 1/2" to 3/4" so just the cookie cutter shape will stand out. Spread some newspaper onto the table. Take old lids from coffee cans or margarine tubs and put just a thin amount of paint in each one. Let the kids dip their "potato stamps" into different colors of paint and stamp the designs onto the bags. Remember to wait for one side to dry before you turn the bag over. Use a hole puncher to put a few holes near the top and string curling ribbon to tie the bag closed after the gift is put in. Or, just fold the top down and staple. You can do this for any occasion. Think how excited the kids will be when they tell the teacher or Grandma that they made the wrappings!

Framed Picture Ornaments

Here's a great project for the kids. Save the shiny metal lids from frozen juice cans. During the year, set aside their best little photos, such as those taken at school or on their birthdays. (Double prints are great!) Take out the photos and cut the images to fit inside the lids. Help them glue some rick-rack, ribbon or lace around the edge, and glue a loop of pretty fabric ribbon to the back...you'll have a Christmas ornament for Grandma and Grandpa. Or, if you'd rather, buy some disk magnets in the craft section and glue them onto the backs of the lids. Then the relatives can look at their little angels all year 'round, every time they open the fridge!

Simmering Citrus Potpourri

1 orange, cut up
1 lemon, cut up
1/4 large cinnamon stick
   or 1-1/2 t. cinnamon

4 bay leaves
1/2 or 1 c. cloves
3 qts. water

Put ingredients in a pan on the stove. Heat until boiling and then simmer on low, low temperature for the rest of the day. Add more water when needed.

Dried Cranberry Heart

To make a dried cranberry heart, use a fine-gauge wire and a strong craft needle to string the cranberries. Then shape the wire into a heart. To make a more substantial heart-shaped decoration, make several strings of cranberries, place them together and tie with twisted pieces of wire. Top with a piece of homespun fabric tied with some sprigs of pine. Hang on the kitchen wall, or above your mantel.

Painted Bucket

A plain metal bucket can be transformed into a lovely container for gift items, potpourri, cookies or pine cones. Simply rub the bucket all over with steel wool to prime the surface. Paint the entire bucket with two coats of enamel, using a wide brush. (You can paint the inside a different color if you wish!) Once the paint is dry, make stencils by tracing shapes onto acetate...stars, gingerbread men, angels...then cutting the shapes out with an artist's blade. Stencil your shapes onto the bucket in contrasting colors. Highlight here and there with a bit of metallic gold paint for extra sparkle!

Bread Dough for Craft Projects

4 c. all-purpose flour　　　　　1 c. salt
　(do not use self-rising)　　　1-1/2 c. hot water

Use this dough to make bread wreaths, potpourri pies, center-pieces, and miniature bread loaves for doll houses. In hot water, dissolve salt as much as possible. Add flour a little at a time. Stir in as you would bread dough until it has the consistency you need to roll out the size for your project. Knead for about 3 to 4 minutes. Store unused portion in a plastic bag in the refrigerator. Bake at 275 degrees for one to 2 hours depending on the size of the object you are making. It must be very hard when completely baked. Cool before decorating or painting. Sometimes it is good to let the piece dry for a few hours. To finish, seal with 2 or 3 coats of clear acrylic. Store in a dry place.

Potpourri Pie

To make a potpourri pie for the stovetop, you will need the following:

basic craft bread dough　　　　peach, cinnamon or berry-
　(recipe is above)　　　　　　　scented potpourri
pie tin　　　　　　　　　　　　green food coloring
lattice pastry cutter　　　　　clear acrylic spray
　(optional)

To bake the top crust, roll out bread dough and cut into lattice strips. Weave the strips together and place over the top of a pie pan. Trim the edges to look nice. To make the rim, roll out the dough in long strips and braid or twist. Wet the edge of the lattice work and "water glue" the finished edge to the lattice. You also may want to make green leaves out of colored dough to garnish the top of your pie. Bake at 275 degrees for about 2 hours and let it dry in the oven for another hour. Make sure the pie crust is hard. When dry, remove the crust and fill the pie tin with potpourri. Using a glue gun, glue the baked top crust to the pie tin. Garnish as desired, and spray with clear acrylic to preserve your pie. Looks and smells as though you always have a freshly baked pie for dinner.

Gingerbread Dough for Craft Projects

3 T. vegetable shortening
1/2 c. sugar
1/2 c. molasses
1 t. baking soda
3-1/2 c. flour
1 t. cloves, ground
1 t. ginger, ground
1 t. cinnamon, ground
3/4 c. water

Use gingerbread dough and your favorite cookie cutters to make gingerbread men garlands, gingerbread ornaments, and gingerbread houses. Heat oven to 350 degrees. Beat the shortening and sugar together until light and fluffy. Stir in molasses. Sift the dry ingredients together. Stir them into the shortening mixture in 3 parts, alternating with a 1/4 cup of water each time. The dough will be stiff. ☆ Refrigerate overnight. Cut the dough into 3 pieces. Knead to warm it slightly, then roll each piece out about 1/4-inch thick. Cut out cookie with a gingerbread pattern of your choice. Use a drinking straw to punch a hole at the center if you plan to hang these ornaments. Place cookies on a baking sheet. Bake for 20 minutes, turn off oven and let them cool. Remove from baking sheet and place them on a rack to dry for about 3 days. Yields about 6 to 10 cookies purely for decorative purposes...not to be eaten! If you wish, you can seal the cookies with three coats of clear acrylic and decorate with colorful acrylic paints when dry.

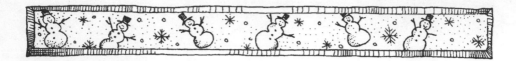

Gingerbread Recipe Wall Hanging

6"x7" piece of white muslin
fusible web
scraps of homespun
approximately 8"x10" dishtowel
   in a pretty check or plaid
black fabric pen
two big buttons
24" piece of twine
7" long tree twig to use as the hanger
gingerbread man (from recipe on previous page)

Bake the gingerbread man out of the basic gingerbread craft dough (p.181). Cut the muslin with pinking shears on all sides. Iron on fusible web to the back of the muslin and also onto the scraps of homespun you are going to use as decoration. Using pinking shears, cut two stars (or hearts) out of the homespun, about 2-1/2 inches wide. These will be used to attach the hanger to the top of the dishtowel. (You can also cut out more homespun stars or hearts to iron on as decoration.) Iron the muslin piece onto the center of the dishtowel. With a fabric pen, print your favorite gingerbread recipe onto the muslin. Use the pen to make little "stitch markings" all around the piece, to make it look as though it is hand sewn. To attach the hanger, iron the stars with the fusible backing at both top corners of the dishtowel. Sew a button into the center of each of the stars. Use twine to tie around both ends of the twig, then wind around the buttons at the top of the dishtowel. With a glue gun, glue the gingerbread man securely to the side at a jaunty angle. Or sew a cookie cutter onto the hanging instead. At last, your very own wall hanging, personalized with your very own gingerbread recipe!

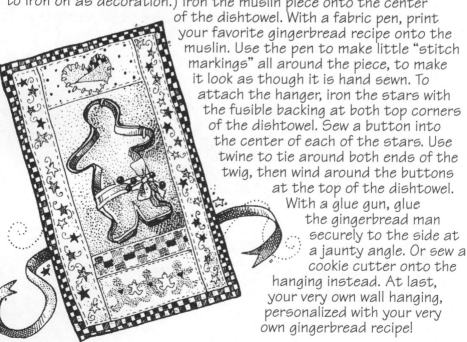

Gift Box Advent Calendar

Here's how to make an Advent calendar for a friend to enjoy! Purchase 24 small, square white gift boxes at a box and mail specialty store. With a big marker, number each box on one side, numbers 1 through 24 (for the days in December that lead up to Christmas). Just for fun, vary the way you number them, using numeric symbols, Roman numerals, writing out the words, using foreign languages, and so on. Purchase small gifts to fit inside each box, such as a fast food gift certificate, socks, small wind-up toys, movie money, special candy... whatever your friend would appreciate. Wrap each item in colorful tissue and slip each into its own box. Seal each box with a holiday sticker. Stack the boxes in order on their sides, with the numbers all facing forward. With a hot glue gun, glue the boxes together, and wrap wide red ribbon around the outside perimeter with a big bow on top. Give the calendar to your friend before December 1 so she can enjoy the anticipation. Each morning from December 1 to December 25, your friend will have the thrill of opening another box.

Candy-Colored Play Dough

2-1/2 c. flour
1/2 c. salt
2 pkgs. unsweetened powdered drink mix
    (orange, cherry, grape, lime, or any flavor)
2 c. boiling water
3 t. vegetable oil

Mix the dry ingredients; then add boiling water and the oil. Stir and mix well. After the dough is cool, mix with your hands and form into a ball. Place in an airtight container. Make lots of different colors for fun projects! Your dough shapes will harden if left uncovered.

Family Fun Surprise Jar

Cut Christmas wrapping paper into 3-inch squares. On the blank side of each square, have family members write ideas for fun things the family can do together during the holidays. Examples might be watching last year's video, sledding, making hot chocolate and popcorn, or driving around looking at Christmas lights. Then fold the papers with the wrapping-paper side showing and place them all in a large jar. Each day agree to draw one idea, then do the activity together. This gives your family some quality sharing time together each day throughout the holiday season. Enjoy, and Merry Christmas!

Photo-Wrap

Make gift wrap out of your family photos. Take your pictures to your local printer and have them copied onto large sheets of paper. Use red raffia as your "ribbon." It's great for small packages! Copy the kids' pictures for Grandma. She'll love it. Print shops can now make full color copies of photos. It's an easy way to add a family photo to your Christmas cards and letters.

Sugarplum Tree

The original sugarplums were whole figs which were transformed into a glazed fruit by long simmering in a sugar syrup. If you'd like to make sugarplum tree, take a cone-shaped form, insert toothpicks all around and place sugarplums (sweets) or gumdrops on each toothpick until the tree is completely covered.

Mistletoe Kissing Ball

A simple version of the Victorian kissing ball is easy to make!

embroidery hoop
satin or velvet ribbon
scissors
white glue
two 4" pieces of thin wire
string or thread
mistletoe and evergreen branches

Separate the inner and outer embroidery hoops. Wind ribbon all around the outer hoop, overlapping the edges as you go. When the whole hoop is covered, cut the ribbon and secure it with a drop of glue. Wrap the second hoop in the same manner. Tuck the smaller hoop inside the larger hoop. Tighten the outer hoop, then secure the top with a piece of wire. Twist a piece of wire around a small bunch of mistletoe. Fasten the mistletoe to hang from the top, inside the "ball." If you're using a large hoop, you may wish to add an evergreen branch to the mistletoe. Slip a loop of thread or string around the top as a hanger. Tie a pretty bow of ribbon at the top, and one at the bottom. Add bells or additional ribbon if you wish. You can keep your mistletoe fresh by storing it in a plastic bag in the refrigerator. Hang the kissing ball near the door, stand under it as guests arrive, and enjoy a Merry Christmas.

Advent Chain

Your child can make an advent chain. Help him or her glue together a paper chain, alternating with red and green construction paper. Make 25 links, and each day beginning December 1st, tear off one link. This will help your child to know how long before Christmas, so the anticipation can build! This little poem can be attached to the top of the chain:

December 1st to Christmas is the longest time of year
Seems as though old Santa never will appear.
How many days to Christmas? It's mighty hard to count
So this little chain will tell you just the right amount.

Easy Christmas Tree Lapel Pin

Here's a fun project for kids...an easy gift they can make! You will need:

assorted fabrics or grosgrain ribbons in pretty holiday colors
a cinnamon stick
a pin back from the jewelry section of a craft store
hot glue
special button

Be sure to select fabrics that have some stiffness and aren't too "floppy." Tear the fabric into small strips approximately 1/4-inch wide. Simply tie the fabric strips onto the cinnamon stick. Once all the fabrics are tied on to suit you, snip the ends so that they're narrow at the top and wide at the bottom, shaped like a Christmas tree. Glue the pin back in place. You can decorate the top of your tree with a pretty gold, silver, or star-shaped button.

Scented Bath Salts

Make your own bath salts in your favorite scents. Use plain rock salt and add a few drops of essential oil. Lavender and rose work really well. Bottle the salts up in pretty jars or other containers for unique and inexpensive gifts. Be sure to make your bath salts a few weeks ahead of time to allow the oil to thoroughly sent the salts. Write a little homemade tag with the simple instructions: Place a few tablespoons of bath salts under the faucet as you draw your bath.

Holiday Candles

Make your own herbal candles for a fraction of what they cost in specialty shops. Purchase pillar candles. Sage green and ecru colors work best. Prepare a mixture of spices such as rosemary, sage and thyme or cinnamon, nutmeg and ground cloves. Melt inexpensive paraffin and dip your candles into the melted wax. Immediately roll them in the desired spice mixture. Using your hands, press the spices into the warm wax. Repeat the process several times to create a nubby-textured candle. A spice candle looks beautiful in a wooden, yellowware or graniteware bowl with bay leaves and rose hips surrounding it.

Forced Bulbs

This is a great winter tradition. If you love to work out in your garden and miss the warm weather, you can get yourself through those wet, cold, gloomy days. Just grow forced bulbs all winter long... narcissus, daffodils, tulips and crocuses. It takes very little effort, and the rewards are wonderful. Look for all sorts of odd containers all year 'round at flea markets and yard sales. Soon your collection will include old pottery bowls, unique granite-ware, terra cotta, and so much more. If you use containers with no drainage hole, be sure and fill the bottom with terra cotta pot shards or gravel. Fill the container with a high quality soil mix (purchased) about 3/4 full. Place the bulbs close together in a shallow container. Sprinkle soil mix around the bulbs to secure them in place. Now comes the fun part! Sprinkle rye grass seed all over the top of the soil. Put a small layer of soil mix on top of the seeds. Water well and put in a fairly cool place. After the shoots are 3 or 4 inches high, your container must be moved to a sunny location. Flowers will develop in a few weeks, and you'll have fresh green grass poking up among the flowers. Really cute to have at Easter too, as an arrangement in the middle of the table with bunnies and colored eggs.

Christmas crafts and recipes can be used all year 'round. Tiny Christmas trees made out of cinnamon sticks and buttons can become a little Valentine tree decorated with button hearts...great favors for a Valentine brunch. The possibilities are endless.

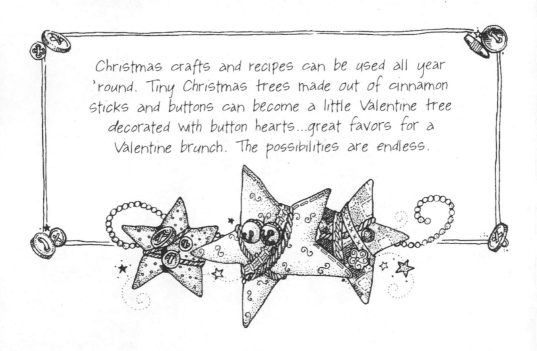

Birch and Grapevine Garland

You can make a garland for your front door out of birch branches and grapevines, and fasten it to the door with hooks. Use several branches and vines woven together for a dense, rather than skimpy, appearance. Weave two strings of tiny white lights in the garland. Design the garland to suit your tastes and the occasion. For a natural theme, weave in long strands of ivy from the garden. (Ivy keeps for about 3 weeks without water.) Add pretty autumn leaves, holly sprigs, dried flowers such as yarrow, cockscomb, and baby's breath, acorns, and strips of homespun. For the holidays, you can also add Christmas ornaments. The branches and white lights are a beautiful combination for any holiday theme. You can keep it all year, adding pumpkins at Halloween!

Outdoor Ice Ornaments

These make interesting outdoor tree decorations as they twist and sparkle in the wind. Line the inside edge of an aluminum pie pan with yarn, leaving enough yarn loose at the top to tie around a tree branch. Fill the tin with water and add berries, flowers and greenery to the water. Place the pans on a level surface in the freezer, or outside if the temperature is below freezing. Freeze the pan until everything inside is frozen solid. Remove the solid piece of ice from the pan (you may have to dip briefly in warm water) and hang outside to enjoy.

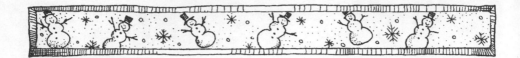

Twinkling Grapevine Spheres

Use up any spare grapevine you may have around. Soak the grapevine in warm water until pliable. Using a large round balloon that is inflated, gently wrap the grapevine around the balloon to form a sphere. Make it as dense or as sparse as you choose. Once the grapevine has dried, pop the balloon. These spheres look really magical wired with tiny twinkling white lights and suspended from bare tree branches.

Christmas Fire Starters

These are so colorful and handy to keep in a basket by the fire. They make a thoughtful gift, too! You will need:

a number of medium-sized pine cones
paraffin or candle stubs
a double boiler
a muffin tin
wicks
red and green crayons
wax paper

Melt the paraffin or candle stubs in the double boiler over hot water. Completely dip each pine cone in paraffin, remove and cool. Pour paraffin 1/2-inch deep into the muffin cups. In each cup, insert a wick about 1-1/2 inches long, so that it will stick out the side. Before the paraffin hardens, press the cones into the cups and allow them to harden. Now you have fire starters. Loosen them from the muffin tin by dipping the bottom of the tin into hot water, removing the starters from the tin. Melt a small amount of additional paraffin in a double boiler and tint it by melting red or green crayons into the paraffin. Let it cool slightly. Dip the bottoms of the cones into the colored paraffin and dry them on wax paper. To use the fire starters, place them under the kindling and light the wick. Note: Use scented candle stubs to add a delicious aroma!

Puff Pastry Wreath

Have fun decorating this easy wreath with cut-outs from your cookie cutters! You will need:

1 pkg. frozen puff pastry
assorted cookie cutters
1 egg white
2 T. water
clear acrylic spray

Thaw frozen pastry according to package directions. On a lightly floured surface, roll out a pastry sheet slightly to soften. Using a sharp knife, cut three one-inch strips the length of the pastry sheet. Join the strips at one end, moistening slightly with water. Braid the strips together and shape into a wreath. Join the ends and overlap them onto the previously joined ends. Using cookie cutters, cut holiday shapes from the remaining piece of pastry and attach them to the wreath as desired. Use a small amount of water to press the shapes on. Make a hole through the top for hanging using a drinking straw. Place your wreath onto a foil-lined cookie sheet. Mix the water and egg white together in a small bowl and brush the entire wreath with the mixture. Bake for 10 to 15 minutes in a 400 degree oven, or until the wreath is golden brown. Cool completely before removing from the cookie sheet. Preserve your handiwork by spraying with several coats of acrylic. If you want to make a larger wreath next time, use both pastry sheets in the package, joining the braided strips to make a bigger circle. Get as creative as you like with the wreath. Leave it a beautiful, golden brown, or add holiday decorations with a glue gun after the wreath has been sprayed and dried. Decorate it with cut-outs of angels, Santas, ornaments, holly leaves and berries...whatever suits your fancy. You can hang it on a nail directly through the hole at the top, or thread some ribbon or yarn through the hole to add color, a bigger hanging loop, and a bow.

Citus and Spice Garlands

The natural beauty of colorful citrus will enhance your holiday home! Dry your citrus slices several weeks before you make your garland. Slice lemons, oranges, and limes crosswise into 1/4-inch slices. Spread the slices out on racks or paper towels to dry, turning frequently. (We don't recommend newspaper, as the ink sometimes transfers to the slices.) When the slices are dry but still pliable and "leathery," string them onto dental floss alternately with whole cinnamon sticks and red wooden beads. Make it as long as you need for hanging across a window. For a different effect, begin with a red wooden bead and string short, uneven lengths of slices, cinnamon, and beads, ending with a loop. Hook the loop directly over a curtain rod, or use ornament hangers to hang it over the rod. String an evergreen garland along the top of the rod to cover the ends of your garland.

Dried Orange and Apple Slices

Use these directions to make lovely dried slices for potpourri, tying on packages, hanging on your tree, decorating wreaths, or embellishing canning jars and other gifts from your kitchen.

Just slice the apples or oranges thinly. Place the slices on a baking sheet lined with parchment paper or lightly sprayed with cooking spray. Heat the oven to 200 degrees and bake for about two hours, until dried. Remove from the oven and continue to let dry for a few days. They look great in canning jars with a pretty cloth lid secured with a piece of twine, or mixed into a basket of potpourri. Just add dried bay leaves and a dried cranberry heart for a beautiful mix.

for the hostess with the mostest

Grapevine Garland

To make a simple grapevine garland for the tree or mantle, buy a number of tiny, 3-inch grapevine wreaths and a bolt of stiff plaid Christmas ribbon from the craft store. Cut the ribbon to make as many 3-inch circles as you have wreaths. When all the ribbon is cut, loop the ribbons and alternate with the wreaths. Use a stapler or hot glue to fasten the ribbon together. Make the garland any length you need. This is just like making a paper chain...it's a fun project to make with children!

Potpourri Sachets

To decorate your country Christmas tree, you can make these easy potpourri sachets. They're very attractive, and they smell great! Choose your favorite fabric according to your theme...country gingham, tiny floral patterns, plaids or checks. Cut the size according to the proportion of your tree; a 4"x6" square will give you about a 3"x4" bag. Put the right sides of the fabric together and just hand or machine stitch up each side and along the bottom. Leave the top unfinished for a more country look. Turn the bag rightside out and fill with potpourri. Tie the top with ribbon or raffia. Attach any type of string or ribbon as a loop for hanging. These simple sachets make thoughtful, unique gifts.

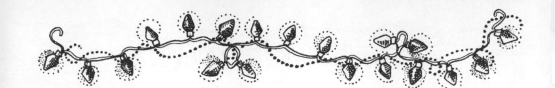

Hurray for the pumpkin pie!

Anonymous

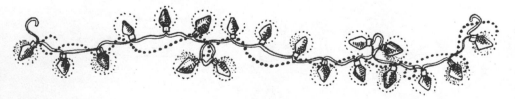

Home for the Holidays

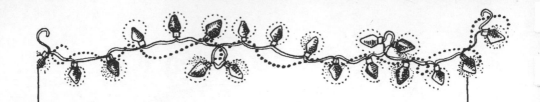

Jolly Little HOW-TO'S

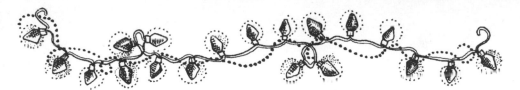

For a festive entrance, pot small live trees, such as Norfolk pines, in straw baskets. Wrap the baskets in big red ribbons and place them by your front door.

Place lots of pure white votive candles in glass holders on the mantel and all over the house to add an overall twinkly light.

Fill a canning jar almost to the top with fragrant potpourri, or with bright red cranberries. Find a clear glass candle holder that will sit nicely on top, inside the rim of the jar. For extra sparkle, use a pure white candle in a votive candle holder.

Look for decorations that light up in many seasonal departments of home stores. Little lighted houses make cheerful nightlights for your children's bedrooms.

Create a lovely centerpiece by building a pyramid of spicy pomander balls...oranges studded with cloves...and sprigs of greenery and berries. Build your arrangement on top of a round wooden cutting board or any flat circular container.

Include a small take-home favor at each place when setting the table for a holiday dinner party. Make your own...even a brightly-decorated sugar cookie will do...or plan ahead and purchase small items at after-Christmas sales.

Use liquid floor wax to add a shine to your fruit centerpieces. Pour the wax into a disposable container and then dip your fruit. Dry on upside down plastic strawberry baskets. Be sure to keep separate from your edible fruit!

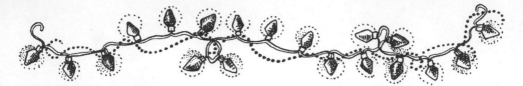

For a really pretty centerpiece, place a white three-wick candle on a round platter. Place individual magnolia leaves flat around the candle with stem end in toward the candle. Alternate golden and red delicious apples on top of the magnolia leaves. Fill around the candle and in between the apples with boxwood and rose hips.

Bundle branches of white pine, cedar, and winterberry and tie them together with raffia for a country touch.

Make heart-shaped waffles with a heart waffle iron. Pierce with a skewer and make a hanger with a piece of twine. Dry your waffles on a rack. String white lights on your tree, then add the waffles and homespun bows. This is a great tree for a kitchen table!

Fill a pair of mittens with potpourri. Join the mittens with a string of yarn, then hang them from a peg near your door for a cozy seasonal look and a welcome scent.

Hang Christmas cookie cutters from red ribbons in your kitchen window.

Display your holiday tins in a cozy nook of your home, and use them for handy items...fill one with holiday napkins, another with ornament hooks, and another with coasters. They make good storage containers, and after the holidays you can nest them and store them easily. It's fun to collect tins at garage sales and antique shops. If you have a friend who collects them, you can add to her collection at Christmas time.

Wrap a fat white candle with cinnamon sticks and tie with a golden bow. Add a sprig of holly.

Tuck silverware into clean, bright mittens at each place setting. Use a scarf as a table runner for a warm winter-time gathering.

Candy canes and silverware tied with a Christmas bow are a surprise greeting at a holiday table.

Mark guests' places with personalized ornaments tied with a bow and placed in wine glasses. Write their names on the ornaments with acrylic paints or a gold or silver pen.

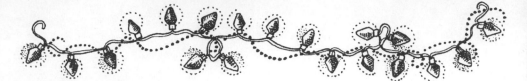

Create a pretty punch bowl filled with iced chamomile tea, citrus spirals (lemon, lime, and orange) and ice cubes containing mock orange or orange blossoms. It looks more beautiful the longer it stands.

A tin grater (new or antique) is transformed into a beautiful container when a votive candle holder and candle are centered underneath. The candlelight makes pretty patterns through the openings. You can tie ribbons or greenery onto the handle to make it even more festive.

To add a mossy appearance to the outside of clay flower pots, clean them with soap and water and dip in a mixture of 2/3 buttermilk to 1/3 water. Leave alone to "grow" outside and they will develop a charming, old-fashioned look.

Tie cinnamon sticks into bundles with a pretty ribbon and use ornament hooks to hang them from the branches of your tree. Six, ten, or twelve-inch sticks work the best.

Use an old flannel shirt to make a Christmas stocking.

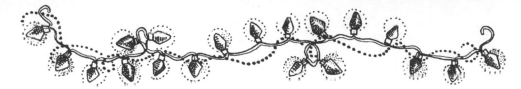

It's so easy to make a cookie cutter kitchen wreath. Buy a plain artificial pine or grapevine wreath, then decorate it with old cookie cutters, cinnamon sticks, dried apple slices and some small bunches of dried baby's breath. Tie everything on with some red raffia. Top off with a pretty plaid ribbon or red raffia bow. Makes the kitchen cheery for the holidays!

Garlands can be as elaborate or simple as you desire, and are very inexpensive to make. When we think of garlands, we often think of pine boughs or braided ivies. But garlands can be made of almost anything...raffia, dried grasses, braided fabric, grape vines, gift wrap, eucalyptus, corn husks, and artificial flowers and greens. You can braid a paper chain out of construction paper, gift wrap scraps, shiny foils or ribbons. Next, add small toys, dried flowers and pods, bunches of cinnamon sticks, and other holiday trinkets and natural items. Of course, your imagination will guide your creative juices. Buttons, bells and beads strung onto ribbon make a charming and unique garland. When hanging a garland on the mantel or shelving, make sure that it hangs evenly (to balance the weight) and that little hands can't reach it to pull it down. Place clusters of candles of different heights in the greens on the mantel, or string some tiny Christmas lights through the garland. If you have a special ornament collection, use a garland to showcase your pieces.

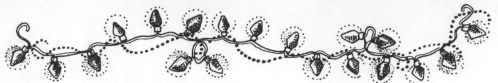

Fill your kitchen with Christmas...decorate a kitchen tree! Use your smallest kitchen utensils, gingham bows and tiny cookie cutters as decorations. Or, try gingerbread cookies and red bows tied with cinnamon sticks. Yet another variation could be fragrant herb bundles, dried flowers, and baby's breath with silk ribbons. Beautiful kitchen tree toppers could be a gingerbread angel or star, a small tin cookie cutter, a chef's hat trimmed with holly and berries, a country crow wearing a Christmas bow, a little wooden spoon angel, or a handmade rag angel made from a new dishcloth. If there isn't room for a kitchen tree, or if very young children abound, consider using a smaller, table-top version...or hang a kitchen wreath using these decorating ideas. It's a fun way to fill your kitchen with the sights and scents of Christmas.

For some good cheer all year 'round, add some special Christmas plants to your garden. Plant holly and red berry trees...you can cut their branches and use them in many home decorating projects. You can also plant pots of different kinds of ivy to use in decorating. Sprigs of ivy are graceful additions to flower arrangements and containers with Christmas berries and holly. Having these plants in your garden enhances your landscape and serves as a supplier for otherwise expensive holiday decorations.

You can use a double wreath hanger on the front door and use the inside hook to hang a child's cherished stuffed toy dressed up with a big Christmas bow and holly sprigs. Dress the cuddly toy as Santa or an angel, or tie a little wreath or wrapped present in its hands or paws. Since it is on the inside of the door, its bows, costume and gift will be protected from the elements.

Here's an easy way to make your house look like Christmas in one afternoon. Take all the pictures off the walls in "company" areas (living room, dining room and guest bath). Wrap each picture like a huge Christmas present, complete with large fancy bows. Rehang all the pictures on the walls in their original spots. This looks especially good with groupings of presents on the wall. For an extra special touch, add large gift tags with Christmas sayings or a few words from a favorite Christmas carol.

So many beautiful cards and gift tags are given each year. Don't throw them away...use them to create your own lovely ornaments and package tie-ons. Cut off the back of the card, and trim around the picture if you wish. Punch a small hole at the top. Spray with a little spray glue and dust with glitter for all-over sparkle. Or, using a glue stick, apply glue around the edges and only on the areas you want to highlight. Sprinkle on the glitter, then shake the excess onto a newspaper. Thread a piece of raffia, twine, or ribbon through the hole, and you have a wonderful tree or garland ornament, or darling package tie-on. Everyone loves to receive a little glitz during the holidays!

Float star-shaped candles among berries and ivy leaves.

Does your tree look "lonely" before and after the presents? Arrange your children's stuffed animals or dolls to sit beneath it until the packages arrive or you take down the tree.

Y ou can use your favorite crystal throughout your home for beautiful holiday decorations. Do you have special glassware that belonged to Grandma or Mom...perhaps some depression glassware or other crystal? Use them throughout the holidays to make wonderful displays with colorful fruit and candles. Share some old memories and make some new ones.

S anta hats everywhere! Try something different this Christmas. Instead of the traditional stockings hanging on the mantel, line up various sizes and styles of Santa hats to hold Christmas treasures. A beautiful arrangement can be made in a large velvet Santa hat using bunches of evergreens, holly, herbs, dried flowers, berries, and pine cones. Stuff the bottom of the hat softly with fiberfill and arrange the natural materials to tumble out of the top in a graceful manner. Hot glue the pieces to make sure everything stays in place. Tack the pompom down near the fur cuff to soften the pointed look of the hat, if desired. You can also hang a hat as a door or wall decoration.

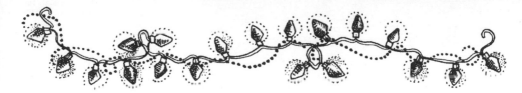

Don't throw away those mismatched mittens or toddler's socks with no mates! Stuffed with a discarded toy or small bouquet of silk flowers, a little lost mitten or sock can become a precious ornament for parents or grandparents. You may want to tuck something inside with a date to remember the size of little hands and feet. Stuff the bottom softly with fiberfill to help define the shape, and glue the treasures into the top.

You can make a beautiful centerpiece with a crystal punch bowl. Put a large candle in the center and decorate around it with pine cones and greenery, or silk poinsettia flowers. A beautiful centerpiece can be made using angel hair as a base in the punch bowl and adding an assortment of your favorite glass Christmas ornaments. The bottom plate of the punch bowl can hold an arrangement of fresh holly or mistletoe to add fragrance to the air.

Don't forget your pets at Christmas. Hang a wreath on the doghouse. How about lights? Put a little jingle bell on Queenie's collar, or a Christmas bandanna around Sammy's neck.

Kitty angels

Make personalized ornaments for everyone in your family with colored glass balls and glitter fabric paints in tubes. Use the paint to write names and messages on the balls, then finish decorating with paint, cording, jewels, sequins and beads. Add a big bow to the top of the ball. At your family Christmas gathering, each person can take a turn hanging his or her ornament. Be sure to make new ornaments for new family members. It's a great way to welcome a new son or daughter-in-law...or baby!... to the family.

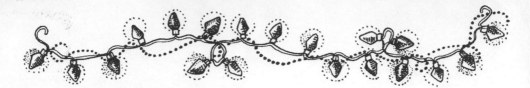

Create an eye-catching Victorian centerpiece by purchasing several old-fashioned footed cake servers at yard sales or flea markets. Stack these three high in the center of your table. (You may want to secure them with a bit of putty.) Fill this tower with fresh fruits such as apples, oranges, plums, and grape clusters draping between the layers. Use walnuts as fillers between the fruit. This makes a stunning old-fashioned fruit tower and looks dramatic in the center of your dining table, in your entry hall or in the living room. Visiting friends will delight in the tower of fresh fruit, and will be pleased to help themselves!

Use antique glass for pretty holiday decorations. For guests, use a tall compote to hold little holiday soaps and an oval relish dish for fingertip towels. Overnight guests will appreciate small candies left on the nightstand in one of your favorite little glass salt dips. Your tiny cordial glasses will look wonderful on the table at each place setting, filled with votive candles, after-dinner mints or candies.

Send a Christmas "care" package to a child who's away at college. Include a small Christmas tree, ornaments, a tape of holiday music, a batch of their favorite holiday cookies...whatever would make their holidays more merry. This is sure to be a big hit!

When everything is cold and snowy, it's so wonderful and festive to have fresh potted flowers growing inside. Narcissus and amaryllis bulbs are plentiful this time of year, and it's amazing to watch their incredible growth...a bit of springtime almost right before your eyes! For a bit of color and good cheer, pick up a Christmas cactus, cyclamen, violets or gloxinia.

Be on the lookout for chandelier prisms at antique shops and flea markets. They make beautiful icicle ornaments for your tree or in the windows, or hanging from a mantelpiece garland.

Make snowballs for your tree or decorating your mantel. Take clear glass ball ornaments and coat with white glue or spray with adhesive. Then roll them in glitter until completely covered and hang the balls to dry. This is a great kids' project!

Green ivy topiaries in terra cotta pots are beautiful and festive. They look terrific lining the mantel or kitchen windowsill.

If you collect antique miniatures, you can use your collections to decorate your house for Christmas. For example, if you collect little houses or log cabins, you can place them among fresh greens on top of a mantel or piano. They'll give you so much pleasure when you can share them with family and friends.

207

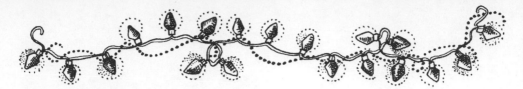

Pick one room in which to do all your Christmas wrapping and crafting. Don't worry about keeping it tidy. Wrap the door to look like a package with a sign that reads "Do not open until Christmas," or "Santa's Workshop," or "Do Not Enter - Authorized Elves Only!"

You can dress up your table for a fancy dinner party by folding cloth napkins into bow ties. Just fold the napkin in half diagonally to form a triangle. Then place the folded edge at the top and, starting at the bottom point, roll up the napkin. Tie a soft knot in the center, and fluff out the ends.

Here are a few ideas for packing cookies safely for mailing. Send only those cookies which can stand jostling. These include the rich moist bars and cake-type drop cookies. To pack bars, line a heavy cardboard box with foil or wax paper. Cut a sheet of cookies to just fit inside the box. Do not cut the bars individually. Place foil or wax paper between layers and on top. Wrap the box with corrugated paper and heavy paper. Mark "Perishable" and "Handle with Care." For cake-type cookies, line a sturdy box with foil or wax paper. Place crumbled paper or a layer of popcorn or puffed cereal in the bottom. Wrap cookies in pairs (back to back), with wax paper between, then wrap the pairs in foil. Pack in rows, snugly. Fill crevices with crumpled paper, popcorn or cereal. Top with a layer of foil and a final layer of crumpled paper. Wrap securely and mark "Perishable" and "Handle with Care." And, if they break after all that, as the saying goes..."that's the way the cookie crumbles!"

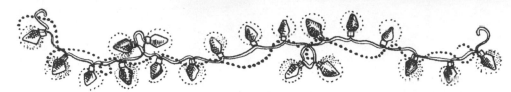

Help your daughter decorate her doll's house for Christmas with tiny wreaths and ornaments.

If a friend or family member has been ill or going through a rough time, buy her a nightgown, some bubble bath or sweet-smelling soap, a candle, and a cassette of soothing music like rainfall, a babbling brook or songbirds. Sprinkle a little potpourri inside the gift packaging. Toss in a bit of angel or teddy bear confetti from a stationery store. Include a teabag, wrapped with the cassette in a little cellophane bag, and a little note telling them to start a cup of tea. Tell them not to open the box until they feel the need to unwind and relax. Call it a "Sanity Package" or a "Stress Relief Box." Let your friend know it is to be used when they're alone and they can enjoy the gift. These packages are a lovely way to say "I love you" or "I care about you." Remember, any gift or package that is wrapped with thought is almost better than the gift inside.

Don't forget to hang a wreath on your birdhouse.

Meet the Gooseberry Friends who contributed to Homespun Christmas...

Peg Ackerman lives with her husband Charlie and son Whit in southern California. Peg has been a frequent contributor to Gooseberry Patch, and loves to decorate her home with fun craft ideas. She creates her own holiday gift wrap and package tags, makes garlands, bakes delicious goodies and collects snowmen. We feel like Peg is an old friend.

Pat Akers also lives in California and has been a valuable contributor to Gooseberry Patch books for a number of years. She has a lot of recipes that were handed down from her grandmother. Pat likes to keep family traditions going, and has passed along some recipes, "as old as the hills," she says, that have been in her family for 40 or 50 years.

Cheryl Berry likes to sew, enjoys crafts and cooking, and loves to find recipes and ideas for almost any occasion that arises. She likes to do cross-stitch for relaxation. Cheryl uses Gooseberry Patch cookbooks quite often, and has contributed many great ideas for the books. Cheryl lives in Florida.

Kathy Bolyea is also from Florida and loves making homemade bread. Since she works full-time, Kathy says "Whoever invented that bread machine is a genius!" Kathy has sent us many great recipes over the years, many of them from her own holiday parties. We really appreciate getting her ideas from the sunny South...sometimes we forget it doesn't snow everywhere!

Judy Borecky has loved cooking and collecting recipes since she was eight years old, and owns about 300 cookbooks. She and her husband have three sons and have lived in Escondido, California for 24 years. Judy enjoys Christmas..."the homecoming of the spirit"...because she enjoys doing for others. She makes her own Christmas ornaments and decorations.

Jeanne Calkins lives in Michigan and has been an herb gardener for the past 15 years. Jeanne is the regional director of a state-wide herb group, and is past president of her local herb group. She enjoys cooking and has a collection of 400 cookbooks. She and her husband have two kids, one still at home, and a cat who "rules the roost."

Nancy Campbell has five children and six grandchildren. Of New England heritage, Nancy lives in a 1920's house in Washington State. She enjoys collecting antique baskets, bean pots, log cabins, bottle brush Christmas trees, crocks, quilts, sheep, snowmen, yellowware and twig furniture. She also likes to go camping and does cross-stitch.

Joy Daniel describes herself as a "30-something year-old kid from Arkansas who loves living in the country, swinging on the porch swing on starlit nights and walking in the woods on crisp fall days." Joy has worked at the local YMCA for many years, and enjoys arts and crafts projects.

Marlene Wetzel-Dellagatta lives in New Jersey. A Registered Nurse, Marlene is employed as a home health aide teacher. Her course includes nutrition and patient care. In her spare time, Marlene enjoys cooking and antiquing. She loves the Christmas season, and has sent in quite a few imaginative ideas.

Jeannine English has shared many excellent ideas with us, including crafts and family recipes. She lives in Texas, and still makes gingerbread houses with her kids, even though they're teenagers now. Jeannine enjoys gardening and especially likes to force bulbs in the dead of winter. She saves precious recipes that have been handed down in her family for generations.

Janice Ertola is from California and is the mother of a boy and a girl. Janice belongs to a "Mom's group" that meets once a month to exchange cookies. Her group also does a homemade gift exchange. Janice and her family host a Sunday brunch for their friends during the holidays each year.

Ann Fehr lives in Pennsylvania and is very active in her community. She is quite busy, as she has two children, ages four and one, and is the national officer for her sorority. Ann also runs a home-based business selling cooking equipment, and has been married for seven years. She enjoys gardening and baking.

Michelle Gardner has a special interest in caring for animals and has contributed lots of tips with furry and feathered friends in mind. She encourages everyone who cares about animals to consider adopting a cat or dog from their local animal shelter. Michelle puts great value in preventing holiday headaches by being organized. She lives in California.

Nancie Gensler is also from California. She collects vintage greeting postcards from the 1920's-40's. Nancie likes to mount her cards in wooden frames that she has painted with a distressed, antiqued look. She has contributed ideas on wrapping with fabric, making garlands, and landscaping with Christmas plants.

Peg Gerch enjoys putting specialized gift baskets together. She sent us some thoughtful ideas for baskets that can be given at Christmas time, for birthdays, or any special occasion. Peg lives in Nebraska. When her sons were young, she used to make up games for them, like "Christmas Bingo," with a homemade playing board and candy pieces as tokens.

Kathy Grashoff is a holiday baker at heart. Her family is originally from Maine, and she has many fond childhood memories of her grandparents. Kathy and family now live in Indiana, and she has five sons. This busy mom loves to cook, likes using her stoneware collection for baking, and has contributed many great recipes to Gooseberry Patch.

Tamara Gruber lives in Texas. As a wife, mother, grandmother, friend and daughter, Tamara believes that "Christmas is a time to explore the best way of showing my love for others." She enjoys creating wonderful Christmas memories for her grandchildren and loves sharing the comforting rituals of tea.

Judy Hand loves to bake and cook. Collecting cookbooks, both old and new, is one of her many passions. She enjoys swapping recipes with friends, and spends many evenings curled up in a chair with a cup of tea, reading her recipe books as if they were novels. Judy lives in Pennsylvania and has contributed lots of great ideas over the past few years.

Glenda Hill lives right in our back yard in central Ohio, and has lived here all of her life. She enjoys reading, crafts, gardening, cooking and baking. Glenda has three cats that she adores. She sent us some good recipes and decorating ideas. We especially like the idea about her grandmother's Christmas pin.

Patricia Husek lives in Michigan and collects old sterling and silverplate silverware. She also enjoys making beautiful gift tags and sewing special handmade items such as Christmas stockings and gift bags made with sentimental bits of fabric and lace. Patricia teaches the sixth grade and enjoys assigning fun art projects.

Judy Kelly has been an elementary school teacher for 27 years, and has taught fifth grade for the last 15 years. She's planning to retire this year. An avid collector, Judy has over 400 cookbooks. She lives in Missouri and has three children, two grand-children and a Black Labrador. She and her family love to go boating and fishing at the Lake of the Ozarks.

Cindy Layton is also from Missouri. She enjoys collecting antiques, cooking, and decorating for all of the seasons. In fact, at Christmas time she decorates four theme trees. Cindy likes walking in the park with her husband, reading and traveling. She works in an office for two orthodontists, and her home is in a country setting.

Barb McFaden is one of our very best contributors. From Montana, Barb is the person in the neighborhood who always hosts the annual Christmas party. Since she loves to entertain, Barb has her home all decked out with country decor and her Santa collection. Many of the recipes she sent in are served at her neighborhood Christmas dinner.

Mary Kathryn Murray lives in Ohio with her husband, two dogs and a cat. She and her husband are busy renovating an 1865 farmhouse. Mary has a degree in interior design, a full-time job, and makes wreaths and basket arrangements in her spare time. She plans to open a shop in their milk house one day with handcrafted items, pottery and antiques.

Wendy Lee Paffenroth lives in a Cape Cod style home with her husband and two teenagers on the land she named Strawberry Hill Farm in upstate New York. She works part-time for an agricultural company, is assistant coach for a championship boys' cross country team, volunteers on the ambulance corps, and has sent us hundreds of yummy recipes.

Marion Pfeifer is an active member of her garden club in Delaware, and has decorated and done flower arrangements as a volunteer for her church and for the Governor's Mansion. She has a Master's degree in Education and has been employed as a teacher. Marion is married and has two sons. Besides gardening, she enjoys cooking, decorating and entertaining.

Jan Sofranko lives on an 11-acre farm in Illinois, and she and her husband are busy restoring their old farmhouse. She enjoys "entertaining on a grand scale," inviting friends over for huge pig roasts. Jan spins wool from the sheep they raise, and also enjoys gardening, crafts, painting, refinishing and recovering furniture, and cooking.

Deb Damari-Tull lives in New York State on an old farm, complete with skating pond and sledding hill. She says her two "rules of thumb" are keeping things simple and natural. September is one of her favorite times of the year, when it's "goodbye to the beach, to the summer, to the garden...a time to anticipate and savor every moment."

Michelle (Shelly) Urdahl lives in Minnesota. She enjoys camping, cross-stitching, stenciling, painting, refinishing furniture and antiquing. A great bargain-hunter, Shelly loves country decorating. She collects rolling pins, cookie cutters, pottery bowls, baskets, dolls, Depression dishes, and "anything gingerbread!"

Yvonne Van Brimmer is a very busy mom with seven children, three still at home. She sews her own clothes, makes doll clothes, collects sheep and enjoys gardening. From California, Yvonne gets satisfaction from doing things the "old-fashioned" way, like making her own bread and soap. Her latest project is learning to make patchwork quilts.

Juanita L. Williams prints her own cookbooks with recipes from family and friends, and has shared many of her favorites. Recently moved to Oregon, Juanita took time out over the holidays to send us a treasure trove of wonderful recipes. This busy single mom of four is a wedding and special events planner who loves Victorian themes and collects Fostoria glass.

Melynna (Mel) Wolk lives in Missouri and is the mother of four kids. She has had many creative positions over the years in the areas of design and advertising. Mel leads a monthly craft group for whom she provides craft projects, complete with illustrated instructions. She volunteers for the La Leche League and enjoys photography and gardening.

Angie Yanchik taught first and second grade for 19 years in the state of Delaware, before she got married and moved to New Jersey. Now working as a kindergarten aide, Angie loves to bake "more than anything else in the world." She comes from a very close-knit Italian family and loves being a homemaker.

Index

weights & measures

3 teaspoons = 1 tablespoon
2 tablespoons = 1 liquid ounce
4 tablespoons = 1/4 cup
5-2/3 tablespoons = 1/3 cup
8 tablespoons = 1/2 cup
12 tablespoons = 3/4 cup
16 tablespoons = 1 cup

8 ounces = 1 cup
16 ounces = 1 pound
1 cup = 1/2 pint
2 cups = 1 pound
2 pints = 1 quart
4 quarts = 1 gallon

☆ Equivalents ☆

Dairy

1 cup cream = 2 cups whipped cream
4 to 5 cups grated cheese = 1 pound
1 cup cottage cheese = 1/2 pound

Eggs

5 eggs = 1 cup
8 to 10 egg whites = 1 cup
12 to 15 egg yolks = 1 cup

Flour & Sugar

4 cups sifted flour = 1 pound
1 cup sifted cake flour = 1 cup flour
              less 2 tablespoons
1 pound sugar, granulated = 2 cups
1 tablespoon cornstarch = 2 tablespoons flour
2 tablespoons arrowroot = 5 tablespoons flour

Butter or Margarine

2 tablespoons = 1 ounce
1/2 cup = 1/4 pound = 1 stick
2 cups = 1 pound

☆ Miscellaneous ☆

1 orange = 6 to 8 tablespoons juice
1 lemon = 3 tablespoons juice
1 orange = 1 tablespoon zest
1 lemon = 1-1/2 to 2 teaspoons zest
1 cup rice = 1/2 pound
1 cup precooked rice = 2 cups cooked rice
1 cup converted rice = 3 to 4 cups cooked rice
1 cup long grain rice = 4 cups cooked rice
1 cup noodles = 1-1/4 cups cooked noodles
1/4 cup macaroni = 1 cup cooked macaroni
1 pound nuts = 2 cups nut meats
1/4 pound chopped nuts = 1 scant cup
1 pound seedless raisins = 3 cups

Temperatures (Fahrenheit)
  32° freezes water
  70° to 75° room temperature
  85° to 100° lukewarm liquid for yeast
  165° to 175° simmer
  212° boils water at sea level
  234° to 240° soft ball from syrup
  244° to 248° firm ball from syrup
  250° to 266° hard ball from syrup
  320° makes sugar liquid
  338° caramelizes sugar
  375° to 400° deep fat frying
  550° broiling

Gooseberry Patch Originals

WELCOME HOME for the HOLIDAYS
your companion from ★ September through December

Welcome Home For The Holidays
from harvest through Christmas, a treasury of holiday recipes, decorating tips, traditions & easy-to-make gifts

Old-Fashioned Country Christmas
A holiday keepsake of recipes, traditions, homemade gifts, decorating ideas, & favorite childhood memories

OLD-FASHIONED COUNTRY COOKIES
hundreds of recipes, tips, & ideas

Old-Fashioned Country Cookies
Yummy recipes, tips, traditions, how-to's, and sweet memories... everything Cookies

OLD-FASHIONED ★ COUNTRY CHRISTMAS our all-time BEST SELLER!

GOOD FOR YOU! recipes, fun ideas, heartwarming stories, good for body, mind, soul

FOR BEES & ME garden-fresh recipes, backyard entertaining & gifts from the garden

For Bees & Me
A Bouquet of Garden-Fresh Recipes, Memories, Hints, Simple Pleasures, Herbal Beauty Potions, Backyard Entertainment & Easy-to-Make Gifts

Good For You!
A collection of good food, good fun, & good stories for the body, mind & soul!

Gooseberry Patch Originals

Reserve your copies today!

Homespun Christmas

Treasured family recipes, memories, homemade decorations, heartfelt gifts & holiday traditions

HOMESPUN CHRISTMAS
A heartwarming collection of Christmas recipes, tips and ideas

Celebrate Spring
BEGIN ANEW

A freshly gathered bouquet of tender recipes, brand new how-tos and tempting tips for the joyous days of springtime.

Celebrate Summer
SUNNY DAYS

A star-spangled collection of luscious recipes, carefree tips and easy how-tos for long, lazy summer days.

Collect the WHOLE SET!

Celebrate Autumn
GIVE THANKS

A bushel of fresh-picked fall recipes, tips & how-to's for the festive season of friends & family.

Celebrate Winter
WELCOMING

A warmhearted collection of recipes for joyful holidays, sparkling celebrations & cozy fireside feasts.

How To Subscribe

Would you like to receive
"A Country Store In Your Mailbox"℠?

Discover the whimsical world of Gooseberry Patch...
hundreds of fun country gifts and accessories, including cookbooks,
Santas, snowmen, ornaments, cookie cutters and so much more!
For a two-year subscription, send $3.00 to:

Gooseberry Patch
149 Johnson Drive
Department BOOK
Delaware, OH 43015
★

Gooseberry Patch
149 Johnson Drive
Department BOOK
Delaware, OH 43015

A Country Store In Your Mailbox®

♡ **How to Order** ♡
For faster service on credit card orders,
call toll free 1·800·85·GOOSE !
(1·800·854·6673)

Please send me the following Gooseberry Patch books:

Book	Quantity	Price	Total
Old-Fashioned Country Christmas		$14.95	
Welcome Home for the Holidays		$14.95	
Old-Fashioned Country Cookies		$14.95	
For Bees & Me		$17.95	
Good For You!		$14.95	
Homespun Christmas		$14.95	
Celebrate Spring		$12.95	
Celebrate Summer		$12.95	
Celebrate Autumn		$12.95	
Celebrate Winter		$12.95	
Coming Home for Christmas		$14.95	
Family Favorites		$14.95	

Merchandise Total _____

Ohio Residents add 6 1/4% _____

Shipping & handling: Add $2.50 for each book. Call for special delivery prices. _____

Total _____

*Quantity discounts and special shipping prices available when purchasing
6 or more books. Call and ask! Wholesale inquiries invited.*

Name: _____

Address: _____

City: _____ State: _____ Zip: _____

We accept checks, money orders, Visa or MasterCard (please include expiration date).
Payable in U.S. funds only. Prices subject to change.

family fun ✿ fireside feasts 🔔 homemade ornaments ✿ making memories 🔔 Grandma's vanilla cookies 🎄 secret presents 🎁 children's giggles ✿ gingerbread men ⭐ festive ribbons 🎀 hot chocolate ☕ Jack Frost on your windowpane ❄ caroling 🎵